Key Figures in Counselling and Psychotherapy

Series editor: Windy Dryden

The *Key Figures in Counselling and Psychotherapy* series of books provides a concise, accessible introduction to the lives, contributions and influence of the leading innovators whose theoretical and practical work has had a profound impact on counselling and psychotherapy. The series includes comprehensive overviews of:

Sigmund Freud
by Michael Jacobs

Eric Berne
by Ian Stewart

Carl Rogers
by Brian Thorne

Melanie Klein
by Julia Segal

Fritz Perls
by Petrūska Clarkson and Jennifer Mackewn

Aaron T. Beck
by Marjorie E. Weishaar

Albert Ellis
by Joseph Yankura and Windy Dryden

Joseph Wolpe
by Roger Poppen

George Kelly
by Fay Fransella

D. W. Winnicott
by Michael Jacobs

J. L.

Moreno

A. Paul Hare and June Rabson Hare

SAGE Publications
London • Thousand Oaks • New Delhi

© A. Paul Hare and June Rabson Hare 1996

First published 1996

SAGE Publications Ltd
6 Bonhill Street
London EC2A 4PU

SAGE Publications Inc.
2455 Teller Road
Thousand Oaks, California 91320

SAGE Publications India Pvt Ltd
32, M-Block Market
Greater Kailash – I
New Delhi 110 048

British Library Cataloguing in Publication data

A catalogue record for this book is available
from the British Library.

ISBN 0 8039 7968 1
ISBN 0 8039 7969 X (pbk)

Library of Congress catalog record available

Typeset by Mayhew Typesetting, Rhayader, Powys
Printed in Great Britain by Biddles Ltd, Guildford, Surrey

Contents

Foreword

Zerka T. Moreno

The history of ideas is replete with struggle, disappointment, frustration and – for a small number of pioneers and proponents – recognition and success. Most met, and continue to meet, with opposition during the beginning stages, often of sufficient proportions as to reduce the bearers of new ideas to the status of isolates. What continues to propel the pioneer is the conviction that his or her particular view of the universe is valid, creative, and necessary for its welfare and future. One aspect of this future contains within itself the possibility that posterity will rediscover these contributions. This is what we mean when we say that pioneers are ahead of their time. Such can be ascribed to many searchers for truth, but searchers with a utopian view belong in a special category: they are, by definition, futurists. Utopia is always to be approximated, never achieved.

One such futurist was J. L. Moreno. His view of the future has not, by any means, come closer to us. Indeed, we may ask ourselves if that vision may ever be realized, even in part. Will there ever be established a world in which every person's choice will count and be made part of the overall decision-making and structure of the world of mankind? It was a view of total inclusiveness. It encompassed the youngest, feeblest, and most ignorant as well as the élite. It was a vision which allowed everyone to be permitted to choose those companions along the way who best fitted one's needs at the moment, dropping all barriers to such choice. It was meant to establish the socio-emotional soil that would allow the growing person to mature closer to his or her potential than was possible under the more restrictive conditions of law and rules extant at the time of that person's arrival in the world. Moreno's vision was that of a "therapeutic world order."

Religion without science, science without religion, and legal codes have failed to deal with the calamities involved in the relationships of human to human. Do all of these compartments hide a dimension previously overlooked? Moreno saw that beneath the formal and informal structure of human society there is another layer, a hidden dimension, which can only be revealed by a method of social microscopy. He postulated that social therapy is analogous to physical medicine in that the outbreak of pestilence on a huge scale is caused by an invisible organism requiring a special instrument, a microscope, to reveal its presence. The body social, too, produces pestilences the sources of which are invisible, but the worldwide effects of which are reflections of these upheavals in small groups.

Sociometry, with its subdivisions, group psychotherapy and psychodrama, were his response to these social ills. For a while, social scientists listened to his voice, then he was absorbed and submerged by the culture. I believe he will be rediscovered. May this book be one of the means by which this is achieved.

Preface

We have been acquainted with Moreno's sociometry, sociodrama, and psychodrama for many years. Paul published his first sociometric study in 1948 (in *Sociometry*) and was introduced to sociodrama while a university undergraduate. In the 1950s and 1960s, on occasion, he would talk with Moreno in the halls during meetings of the American Sociological Association and listen while Moreno recounted his experience of sitting in the branches of a tree in the garden in Vienna while children enacted the stories he told. In 1954 when a bibliography of small group research was published in Moreno's journal, *Sociometry*, Moreno contributed references for his own work which he judged to be significant contributions (see Strodtbeck and Hare, 1954).

June was introduced to psychodrama at the Sixth International Congress on Psychodrama and Sociodrama in Amsterdam in 1971. She decided to combine her interest in group work as a social worker with her professional experience as an actress and singer by studying psychodrama, first by reviewing the literature and then, in 1974, by beginning her training to become a psychodrama director with Zerka Moreno, Ann E. Hale, and John Nolte at the Moreno Institute, Beacon, New York. J. L. Moreno had died a few months before and Zerka was continuing the traditional training. Paul joined in the training experience, eventually to become a qualified "auxiliary ego". In those days June and Paul lived in South Africa in Cape Town, some considerable distance from Beacon, where training was available.

June and Paul returned to Beacon in 1977. While June participated in and directed psychodramas downstairs, Paul in a third floor room at the Institute read selections of Moreno's work that were suggested by Zerka Moreno and used the basement library to begin to collect references for a complete bibliography of Moreno's work. At Zerka's suggestion we had the intention of finding a publisher for a collection of Moreno's most significant articles summarizing his theory and method, examples of psychodramas he directed, and critiques of his work that had been published. Although we were not successful in finding a publisher for this collection at that time, all of the material has found its way into the present volume, some as direct quotes and some in the form of summaries of articles or passages from books. Just as Zerka was a facilitator for J. L. Moreno during his life, to assist in the presentation of his ideas, so she also played the role of facilitator for us by providing a list of Moreno's most significant works and examples of his practice of psychodrama.

June's research for her Master's Thesis in Social Work at the University of Cape Town involved the comparison of the effectiveness in the use of psychodrama with role-playing in the treatment of alcoholics in a residential treatment center. She completed her training as a psychodrama director at the Moreno Institute and was certified as a Trainer-Practitioner by the American Board of Examiners in Psychodrama, Sociometry, and Group Psychotherapy in 1990. In 1996 she was honored by the American Society of Group Psychotherapy and Psychodrama by being awarded a certificate as a Fellow of the Society. She has taught psychodrama and the use of psychodramatic techniques and used psychodrama in group therapy in South Africa, the United States, the United Kingdom, and Israel. In Israel she was one of the founders of the Israeli Psychodrama Association.

Paul has never practiced psychodrama nor served as an "auxiliary ego" in any therapeutic enterprise. However he found an opportunity to publish some of the materials, originally intended for the Moreno anthology, in other forms. A short version of Moreno's biography was published in 1979, the complete bibliography of his writing in 1986, and the description of Moreno's sociometric study at the Hudson School for Girls, which is included here in Chapter 3, in 1992. Summaries of sociometric research appeared in handbooks of small groups research in 1962 and 1976 and a form of dramaturgical analysis of social behavior, based in part on Moreno's ideas, in books in 1985 and 1988.

Given our interest in Moreno and his work, over the years, Windy Dryden's series on the contributors to counseling and psychotherapy provides us with an incentive to review Moreno's work and to present it to a new audience. Windy Dryden gave helpful comments on the organization of this volume.

In addition to providing the impetus for the present work, Zerka Moreno read the present manuscript, noting both corrections and additional insights into Moreno's life. Some of her additions are included in the text and others appear as footnotes. We are also thankful that Jonathan Moreno was able to clarify some points concerning his father's life. Grete Leutz, Ed Borgatta (who also edited the journal *Sociometry*) and Ann Elizabeth Hale, who were trained by Moreno, added their perspectives as well as Peter Felix Kellermann who was trained by Zerka and is a practicing psychodramatist. Adam Blatner, psychiatrist and psychodramatist, contributed his own insights concerning the importance of various aspects of Moreno's work. Psychologists Dean Peabody and Herbert Blumberg provided comments. Some persons who knew Moreno mainly as a social scientist, Henry Meyer, Leonard Cottrell, Theodore Newcomb, and especially Wellman Warner, made their contributions in 1978, or earlier, and it is only now that we are able to show our appreciation in print. Two readers of drafts of the manuscript, Barbara Rosenstein and Carol Troen, who were not familiar with Moreno's work, gave their impressions of the way members of a lay audience might receive the book. Although Rene Marineau did not read our manuscript, we read his book on the life of Moreno (1989) many times. Our first chapter draws heavily on the material in Marineau's detailed biography.

Special thanks to Susan Worsey as Counselling Commissioning Editor, Rosemary Campbell, as Book Production Editor and Derek Todd, as Production Controller for Sage Publications, who were most helpful in seeing the manuscript through the press.

A. Paul Hare
June Rabson Hare

Acknowledgments

We wish to thank the following publishers and holders of copyrights for giving permission to reprint selections of Moreno's work or descriptions of his work.

American Society of Group Psychotherapy and Psychodrama for material from J. L. Moreno, "Fragments of the psychodrama of a dream", *Group Psychotherapy*, 3(4): 344–64, 1951; J. L. Moreno, *Who Shall Survive?* Beacon Press, Beacon, NY, 1953. Copyright © 1953; J. L. Moreno, "Comments [on the history of psychodrama]", *Group Psychotherapy*, 11(3): 260, 1958; J. L. Moreno, *Psychodrama: First Volume*. Beacon House, Beacon, NY, 1972. Copyright © 1972; J. L. Moreno, "The function of the social investigator in experimental psychodrama", *Group Psychotherapy and Psychodrama*, 26(3–4): 7–30, 1973; J. L. Moreno, "Autobiography of J. L. Moreno", *Journal of Group Psychotherapy, Psychodrama and Sociometry*, 42(1), 1989; J. L. Moreno and Z. T. Moreno, *Psychodrama: Third Volume*. Beacon House, Beacon, NY, 1969. Copyright © 1969. Routledge, International Thompson Publishing Services for material from W. J. Warner, "Sociometry and psychiatry", *British Journal of Sociology*, 5(3): 228–37, 1954. Reprinted by permission. Helen Dwight Reid Education Foundation for material from A. P. Hare, "Moreno's sociometric study at the Hudson School for Girls", *Journal of Group Psychotherapy, Psychodrama and Sociometry*, 45(1): 24–39, 1992. Reprinted by permission of the Helen Dwight Reid Education Foundation. Published by Heldref Publications, 1319 18th Street, NW, Washington, DC 20036-1802. Copyright © 1992. Tavistock/ Routledge for material from R. F. Marineau, *Jacob Levy Moreno, 1989–1974*. Tavistock/Routledge, London, 1989. Copyright © 1989. Springer Publishing Company for material from A. Blatner and A. Blatner, 1988, *Foundations of Psychodrama*. Springer Publishing Company, Inc., New York 10012. Copyright © 1988.

1
The Life of J. L. Moreno

Jacob Levy Moreno (1889–1974) had a revolutionary goal to change society by bringing together individuals capable of harmonious interpersonal relationships to create social groups that could function with maximum efficiency and with minimum disruptive processes (1934: xii). To do this he sought a "technique of freedom, a technique of balancing the spontaneous social forces to the greatest possible harmony and unity of all" (1934: 7).[1]

The concept of "role" was central to Moreno's theory and he played many himself. He was a psychiatrist, dramatist, theologian, poet, philosopher, inventor, group psychologist, psychodramatist, sociodramatist, sociometrist, sociatrist, and educator. Although he made significant contributions in all of these roles, the three areas in which he was most creative, and that have had a major impact on the theory and practice of social science and group psychotherapy, are psychodrama, sociodrama, and sociometry. For Moreno, each of these methods was a contribution to the overall process that would make it possible for men and women to realize their God-like creative potentials and thus fashion a world in which true liberation was possible.

Moreno saw all of his work as part of a "sociometric movement" (1953: xiii) that was not simply the measurement of feelings and perceptions of positive and negative relationships between group members (which is the more limited meaning of "sociometry"), but included group dynamics, group psychotherapy, role playing, interaction research, psychodrama (enactment focusing on personal issues), and sociodrama (enactment focusing on social roles and social issues). He divided the development of this "movement" into several periods (1953: xiv):

1911–23: The formative period for his ideas, including his experiences as a philosophy student, and later as a medical student, and with the spontaneity theater in Vienna.
1923–34: Beginning with the publication of the first German edition of his book on the spontaneity theater and ending with

the publication of the first edition of *Who Shall Survive?* (1934). During this period he carried out his most extensive sociometric research at the Hudson School for Girls in New York State.

1937–42: From the launching of the journal *Sociometry* to the opening of the Sociometric Institute and the New York Theater of Psychodrama. By the end of this period, Moreno was 53 years old and in the midst of a very productive phase.

1942–74: During these years Moreno traveled widely, spreading his ideas about group psychotherapy, psychodrama, sociodrama, and sociometry throughout the world.

The account of Moreno's life given here follows this general outline, except that the story begins with Moreno's birth and some childhood experiences which introduce themes that were to reappear throughout his life. Note is also taken of the roles of the women who served as his support and inspiration. On occasion, we quote Moreno directly to let him tell a story or explain his ideas in his own words. Our role is thus similar to a psychodrama director who facilitates the "self-presentation" of the protagonist.

An eventful life

Moreno was born in Bucharest, Romania, on 18 May 1889, the son of Moreno Nissim Levy and Paulina Iancu, both descendants of Sephardic Jewish families. At the time of their marriage, Moreno's father was 32 years old, a relatively poor traveling salesman. Moreno's mother was 14 years old when she accepted her older brother's choice of a husband. One day she was a schoolgirl in a Catholic convent, where she was exposed to French language and culture and Christian values, and the next day a wife, living by herself, while her husband traveled in the Balkans selling "Turkish wares."

Although Moreno's mother reports that he was born under more ordinary circumstances, he has claimed that he was born on a ship that was traveling the Black Sea, and thus began life as a wanderer and a citizen of the world. He was the oldest of six children, with three sisters and two brothers. His family lived in Romania for five years after he was born and then moved to Vienna.

Marineau (1989: 12) stresses two points concerning Moreno's background. The first is the influence of his mother's French upbringing as evidenced in the names given to the children (for example, Jacob was always referred to as Jacques in the family). Secondly, that the last name of Levy was gradually replaced by the name Moreno. Jacob was the first one to use his father's first name as a family name and almost everyone in the family besides his father and sister Charlotte followed his example. Thus, by appropriating his father's first name, Jacob could claim to be establishing a new dynasty. Moreno added his own comment to the discussion of his name (Moreno, 1958: 260):

> The name Moreno has often been taken as a Spanish or Italian name. Neither assumption is correct. I am a Sephardic Jew. I am not the son of a rabbi although there have been rabbis in my ancestry. My father's name was originally Morenu Levy; Morenu is the Hebrew word meaning "our teacher." He changed Morenu to Moreno, and my name became J(acob) L(evy) Moreno.

Moreno had a special relationship with his mother and with those around him (Marineau, 1989: 15). When he was 12 months old he had a severe attack of rickets. One day, when his mother had taken him out to the yard, a gypsy passed by who suggested placing the baby on hot sand at high noon so that the sun would heal him. The gypsy also added a prophecy that he would become a very great man and that people would come from all over the world to see him. From that day his mother believed that God had given her a special mission to reinstate his health and prepare him for his future.

When he was four and a half years old he had his first experience of playing God as part of a game while his parents were away. This was the first of a series of incidents that Moreno felt revealed the main themes of the work in his adult years (1972: 2):

> When I was four and a half years old my parents lived in a house near the river Danube. They had left the house on Sunday to pay a visit, leaving me alone in the basement of the house with the neighbors' children. The size of this basement was about three times the size of an average room. It was empty except for a huge oak table in the middle. The children said: "Let's play." One child asked me: "What?" "I know," I said, "let's play God and his angels." The children enquired: "But who is God?" I replied, "I am God and you are my angels." The children agreed. They all declared: "We must build the heavens first." We dragged all the chairs from every room in the house to the basement, put them on the big table and began to build one heaven after another by tying several chairs together on one level and putting more chairs above them until we reached the ceiling. Then all the children helped me to climb up until I reached the top chair and sat on it. There I sat pretty. The children began to circle around the table, using their arms as wings, and singing. Suddenly I heard a child ask me: "Why don't you fly?" I stretched my arms, trying it. A second later I fell and found myself on the floor, my right arm broken. This was, as far as I can recall, the first "private" psychodramatic session I have ever conducted. I was the director and the subject in one.

Moreno's God-playing games were repetitive and fully supported by Moreno's mother. Moreno noted that in later years he was often asked why the psychodrama stage was constructed in the three-tiered form with a balcony.

The first inspiration may have come from this personal experience. The heavens up to the ceiling may have paved the way towards my idea of the many levels of the psychodrama stage, its vertical dimension, the first level as the level of conception, the second the level of growth, the third the level of completion and action, the fourth – the balcony – the level of the messiahs and the heroes. The warming up to the difficult "role" of God may have anticipated the warming up process through which subjects have to pass in the process of spontaneous role acting on the psychodrama stage. That I fell when the children stopped holding up the chairs may have taught me the lesson that even the highest being is dependent upon others, "auxiliary egos," and that a patient–actor needs them in order to act adequately. And gradually I learned that other children too, like to play God. (1972: 3)

Although Moreno was close to his mother, Marineau feels that the most important relationship in Moreno's life was with his father (1989: 17–18). Even though his father was away from home much of the time, young Jacob still loved and idealized him and sided with him against his mother and uncles. Marineau concluded that Moreno incorporated his father, thus reinforcing a tendency toward megalomania, since the inner representation of "the father" took on a mystical aspect that would later be confused with one of God. Soon after entering school, he confirmed his identification with Father–God by refusing to be called by his given name, even by his brothers and sisters: nobody, he said, calls God by his name.

When Moreno was six or seven years old, his family moved to Austria where his father worked for a company in Vienna. Moreno went to school in Vienna where he rapidly became a favorite pupil because of his curiosity and intelligence. Although his family did not emphasize their Jewish identity, Moreno had a bar mitzvah at the Sephardic temple in Vienna.

He was 14 years old when his parents migrated once more, this time to Berlin. Moreno cites as evidence of his father's devotion to him the fact that a tutor was employed, at a financial sacrifice, to teach Moreno Latin for the examination he had to pass to enter the fourth class at the Berlin Gymnasium. However, Moreno was unable to adjust to German culture and schooling, and moved back to Vienna.

At about this time, Moreno traveled through Italy with one of his uncles. He met a young and beautiful woman in Florence named Pia and immediately fell in love. Marineau (1989: 21) records that

Pia was the first girl to become Moreno's "muse," replacing his mother as the person who would motivate him to surpass himself.

His parents became separated, leaving Moreno angry and depressed; the formerly well-behaved student now argued with his teachers and missed classes. Later, he quit the Gymnasium without completing his "matura." During his school vacation, he visited his family in Chemnitz, a provincial German city where they then lived. One night, while standing in front of a statue of Jesus Christ in a park, he had the inspiration that he was indeed an extraordinary person and that he had been placed on the planet to fulfill an extraordinary mission. Having been through a period of revolt in which he wished to destroy the world, he now wanted to build a new one.

Early professional years in Vienna (1909–25)

Prior to entering university, Moreno spent two years of intense soul-searching (Marineau, 1989: 26–30). He was trying to find the mission that he felt God wanted for him. He read many books with no supervision. One day he saw himself as a servant of God, the next as a replica of the Almighty, and even as God himself. Throughout, he remained convinced that action was more important than words, experience a better teacher than books.

He entered the University of Vienna in 1909. He had been seen around the faculty for some time, dressed in a green cloak of the kind worn by Austrian peasants. He went without a hat and let his beard grow. When another student, Chaim Kellmer, approached him one morning, the two young men felt an immediate rapport and an enduring friendship developed. Chaim would visit the Moreno family, acting as an intermediary between Jacob and his mother. Moreno's mother complained to Chaim that she wished Moreno would not be so eccentric. Chaim would accompany Moreno to the park and join in playing with the children.

Together they founded a group called "The Religion of Encounter" and established a community based on its principles. Three more students joined the house which was open to new immigrants and refugees. Their sign read: "Come to us from all nations and we will give you shelter." Newcomers were helped to fill out papers and apply for official documents and find jobs. Every night there were discussions about practical problems, and a great deal of singing and fun.

The group as a whole adopted a policy of anonymity. All would abandon their names, following an old Christian tradition that had the meaning of sharing everything in the name of charity. Moreno recalled (1989a: 34):

> My new religion was a religion of being, of self-perfection. It was a religion of helping and healing, for helping was more important than talking. It was a religion of silence. It was a religion of doing a thing for its own sake, unrewarded, unrecognized. It was a religion of anonymity.

Moreno assumed the role of leader, but the House of Encounter was closed at the beginning of the First World War and the five members of the group went separate ways. Chaim Kellmer died of tuberculosis during the war.

Moreno's entrance to the University of Vienna was complicated by the fact that he had left school before obtaining his "matura" and could not enter the Faculty of Medicine. He was admitted first in philosophy under a temporary status until he had taken written and oral examinations. From 1909 to 1910, he took traditional courses in philosophy, while also registering for classes in the Faculty of Medicine. In 1910, he transferred to the Faculty of Medicine to start the first of ten semesters. While in medical school, Moreno came to the attention of Dr Otto Pötzl, head of the Clinic of the Neuropsychiatric Department, and was made an assistant there. The association with Pötzl gave Moreno a chance to work in the university clinic and at a psychiatric hospital, his first experience of institutions for the mentally ill.

In 1911, while a university student, Moreno had another set of experiences which reinforced his idea that he could be a creator. He said, "I took to anonymity, spontaneity and creativity like wood takes to fire and began my Godplaying in the streets and gardens of Vienna." He tells the story:

> One day I walked through the Augarten, a garden near the archduke's palace, where I saw a group of children loafing. I stopped and began to tell them a story. To my astonishment other children dropped their games and joined in, nurses with their carriages, mothers and fathers and policemen on horseback.
> From then on one of my favorite pastimes was to sit at the foot of a large tree in the gardens of Vienna and let the children come and listen to a fairy tale. The most important part of the story was that I was sitting at the foot of the tree, like a being out of a fairy tale and that the children had been drawn to me as if by a magic flute and removed bodily from their drab surroundings into the fairy land. It was not as much what I told them, the tale itself, it was the act, the atmosphere of mystery, the paradox, the unreal become real. I was the center, often I moved up from the foot of the tree and sat higher, on a branch; the children formed a circle, a second circle behind the first, a third behind the second, many concentric circles, the sky was the limit. (1953: xviii)

Moreno, indeed, seemed to feel that the sky was the limit and that he held his power by "the grace of God." He was conscious of an *idée fixe* to leave the world of children and test the "living God idea" within the framework of society. He concluded that *"the only way to get rid of the 'God syndrome' is to act it out."* Moreno's direct and confrontational approach led him to further activity. One day in 1911 he entered a theater with a friend when the play being presented was *Thus Spake Zarathustra*, based on Nietzsche's book of that name. Moreno stopped the actor who was playing the role and objected that nobody but Zarathustra himself could play the role. The director of the play and the author came to the defense of the actor. Moreno then announced that they were witnessing the end of traditional theater and that the time was ripe for the birth of the only real theater in which every actor would play him or herself and not a role. The police were called and Moreno and his friend were taken before a judge where they promised not to interfere with other people's plays. This is only one version of the story; in another version, the incident occurs while Moreno is putting on a play for the children in the Augarten. This story was the basis for the publication of the article "The Godhead as comedian or actor" published in *Daimon* in 1919 (Marineau, 1989: 45–6).

Moreno liked to recall his early encounters with people who were influential or were influenced by his own ideas. He describes his meeting with Freud as follows (1972: 5–6):

I met Dr Freud only on one occasion. It occurred in 1912 when, while working at the Psychiatric Clinic in Vienna University, I attended one of his lectures. Dr Freud had just ended his analysis of a telepathic dream. As the students filed out he asked me what I was doing. "Well, Dr Freud, I start where you leave off. You meet people in the artificial setting of your office, I meet them on the street and in their home, in their natural surroundings. You analyze their dreams. I try to give them the courage to dream again. *I teach people how to play God.*"

Dr Freud looked at me as if puzzled. But psychoanalysis had developed an atmosphere of fear among young people. Fear of neurosis was the measure of the day. It was psychoanalysis which began the fight against genius from the rear, to reproach and distrust him because of his complexes. After purging nature (Darwin) and society (Marx) from creative cosmic forces, the final step was the purging of genius by psychoanalysis. It was the revenge of the mediocre mind to bring everything down to its lowest common denominator. As everyone has complexes and as the creative man is no exception, all men are alike. All men are geniuses, the one makes an effort to be, the other doesn't care. An army of Philistines fall over Samson. He was admired and feared for no reason. He was not stronger than we are, it is only the complex, the long hair. Everyone can let his hair grow.

While Moreno was at the University of Vienna, there were demonstrations, celebrations, and fist fights between members of different political movements, including those he identified as "Nazis," the communists, and the existentialists. Moreno associated himself with the existential movement. For Moreno, the principles of the three movements were clear. The Nazis proposed to conquer the world for the Germans so they could rule it. The communists wanted to conquer the world for the working class. The early existentialists emphasized, in contrast, existence itself as something sacred. Whenever they saw existence threatened, they tried to restore it in its native form against the invasion of the robot (1989a: 47–8). The first principle of the existential movement was all-inclusiveness and the second the goodness of all existing things, and above all the idea of spontaneity and creativity of the moment, the urgency of their immediate experience.

The year 1913–14 is given by Moreno as the genesis of group psychotherapy, which developed in parallel with the idea of acting out. Again Moreno tells a story:

> One afternoon I walked through the Praterstrasse when I encountered a pretty girl smiling at me. She wore a striking red skirt and white blouse with red ribbons to match it. I had hardly begun to talk to her when a policeman came between us and took her away. I followed and saw them entering a police station. After a while she came out and I asked her what had happened. "Well," she said, "they told me that we are not permitted to wear such striking clothes as this during the day, as we may attract customers. It is only after sundown that we are allowed to do so." (1953: xxviii–xxix)

Moreno continues the story by noting that Vienna at the time had a red light district, a ghetto for prostitutes who were segregated from the rest of society because of their occupation. He began to visit their houses, accompanied by Dr Wilhelm Gruen, a specialist in venereal disease, and Carl Colbert, the publisher of a Viennese newspaper, *Der Morgen*. Moreno says that his visits were not motivated by a desire to reform or analyze the girls, nor to find the "charismatic prostitute." Rather he wanted to help make them respectable, to give them dignity, and he decided to begin with the therapeutic aspect rather than the economic.

Moreno and his companions started to meet groups of eight to ten girls, two or three times a week. They met in the afternoon at tea time and discussed everyday incidents in their lives: being arrested, having venereal disease, and becoming pregnant. At first the girls were fearful, but gradually they began to open up when they saw some benefit in the meetings. A lawyer was found to represent them in court and a doctor to treat them. Gradually, they found ways to help each other. Money was contributed for the expenses of the meeting and for emergencies such as sickness. Although it may have looked from the outside like a prostitute "union," Moreno began to see that one individual could become a therapeutic agent for another and the potentialities of a group psychotherapy on a reality level crystallized in his mind.

Another of Moreno's pastimes during his medical student days was to go to the courts and witness trials. He would then return home and, with his friends or family, reconstruct the drama of the trial. He would play all the different roles, including judge and jury. On this basis, he would predict the outcome of the trial, giving reasons why a lawyer might fail or why a witness was convincing. His friends would wait for the outcome of the trial and note the high percentage of correct predictions that Moreno had made (Marineau, 1989: 40).

The period of the First World War found Moreno moving away from his religious ecstasies to more normal conduct. His intimate circle of enthusiasts had disbanded and his friend, Chaim, had died. He volunteered for military service in 1914, but was not permitted to serve because his citizenship status was not clear. From his father he had inherited both Turkish and Romanian nationality and his family had never obtained Austrian citizenship.[2] However, as an advanced medical student with considerable clinical experience, he was hired by the government as a medical officer. For the first time in his life he had plenty of money. His first assignment was Mitterndorf, a refugee camp (1989b: 63).

Mitterndorf refugee camp

From 1915 to 1917 Moreno, first as an advanced medical student and then as a young doctor, held the posts of superintendent and medical officer at a refugee camp in Mitterndorf for Austrians of Italian extraction who were fleeing from the South Tyrol because of invasion by the Italian army. Thousands of people had left their homes and needed to be temporarily housed. They were quartered in barracks, each accommodating up to one hundred people who were not free to leave the camp. When Moreno arrived, there were more than 10,000 people living in the camp, mostly old people, women, and children. As more people arrived they were placed in the next empty barrack. Moreno was assigned to the children's hospital in the camp.

He started to observe the living conditions of the people in the barracks and made his first observations of the importance of interpersonal bonds for a viable community. People from different villages had been thrown together without any selection process. Many were from the mountains and unaccustomed to the environment. Moreno studied the psychological currents that developed around differences of nationality, politics, sex, and staff versus the community members. These factors he considered the chief contributory sources of flagrant maladjustments and disturbances. He counted the experience as one of the highlights of his career since it provided the insight that a sociometrically planned community might be possible.

Moreno returned to Vienna to finish the work for his MD degree which he received in February of 1917 from the University of Vienna. At the ceremony, the dean of the faculty told his mother "Your son is a great genius. He has a great future" (1989b: 69).

Bad Vöslau and Marianne

From 1918 through 1925, Moreno served as public health officer in Bad Vöslau, Austria, a spa resort in a wine-growing region in the environs of Vienna. This was an unusual position for a Jew in the Austria of his day. In addition, he was the medical director of one of Austria's largest cotton mills which was located in the city and was also engaged in private practice in Vöslau and Vienna.

In Bad Vöslau, Moreno did not charge the people of the town for his services since he was already receiving salaries as health officer of the town and as medical director of the local textile mill. He made himself available at all times, especially to the poor. However, his skills did not extend to delivering babies, so he made an arrangement for this part of his practice with another doctor in the town.

Marineau (1989: 58) recounts that shortly after Moreno arrived in Bad Vöslau he met Marianne Lörnitzo. She was a Catholic, dedicated to her family, engaged to a young man from the town, and a school teacher. When Moreno saw her on the street, he loved her at first sight. A few weeks later, when she came to consult him for a minor medical problem, they felt drawn to each other. She soon became his medical assistant, his secretary, his lover, and above all his inspiration, his "muse." Not since his infatuation with his mother and his platonic romance with Pia had Moreno felt this kind of love. Marianne moved into the house with Moreno.

Moreno felt that the relationship was not a typical love affair. In his *Autobiography* (1985, ch. 7: 8, cited by Marineau, 1989: 61), he wrote that he really wanted to find a woman who would put up with his fantastic utopian ideas, one who would love him both physically and spiritually, a muse. Since Moreno felt that he was both a man and a God-player, he wanted to find a woman who could be a man's lover and also be a God-player's lover. He had heard the name given to such a woman, Muse, the goddess or the power regarded as the source of inspiration to the poet.

Moreno had heard voices as a child, but always kept it a secret thinking that people might find him "abnormal" (Marineau, 1989: 62). However, he shared this secret with Marianne, who shared some of her own inner voices, and after a while they both heard voices. Their lives revolved around this "inner and mutual experience." In Moreno's words: "I suddenly felt reborn. I began to hear voices, not as a mental patient does, but as one who feels that he can hear a voice that reaches all beings and speaks to all beings in the same language . . . that . . . gives us hope, gives us direction, gives our cosmos direction and meaning." One day, in a mood of complete inspiration, he rushed into the house. "The only thing I heard was a voice, words, words, coming, going through my head. I didn't have the patience to sit and write them all down. I grabbed one red pencil after another, went into the top room of the house near the tower and began to write upon the walls." The words on the wall were in the form of a poem that begins:

O open yourself
Valley of May
To the One who created you.

Moreno waited with Marianne to hear the voice again and then one night they heard it, as if God was communicating to them from infinite horizons. This led Moreno to begin a long poem, first published in *Die Gefahrten* and by Kiepenheuer Verlag in 1920 as *Das Testament des Vaters* and later as *The Words of the Father* (1971: 49–57). The poem begins:

I am God
The father
The creator of the universe
These are my words
The words of the father

When Moreno moved to Bad Vöslau he started to use the given name of his father, Moreno, with his own name and he signed himself Jacob Moreno Levy. Marineau (1989: 66) suggests that in the poems that Moreno published, including *The Words of the Father*, there is a symbolic attempt to become his own father and that he was calling on readers to believe that they would become self-fulfilling only when they took responsibility for their own creativity and involvement in the cosmos.

The poem also represents Moreno's ideas about religion. In Bad Vöslau he recreated the religion of encounter and had his own followers. He apparently confronted a Catholic priest in front of a church and said he should preach on the street. Later, he published the story in "The Godhead as preacher" (1919). The incident had the effect of isolating him and Marianne from the majority of the community. The poem has also raised questions about Moreno. Some of his disciples see it as the most important work he ever wrote, others are uneasy about it. His enemies quote it as proof of his lack of mental equilibrium (Marineau, 1989: 66–7).

Another set of events anticipated Moreno's development of psychodrama. A wealthy man, who came to Moreno as a patient, wanted Moreno to help him die and was ready to include Moreno in his will. Moreno made it clear that as a doctor he was there to make people feel better about themselves. For weeks they talked about the different ways of committing suicide and acted out different scenarios with the help of Marianne. Moreno used a similar approach with other families, re-enacting difficult situations, either in his office or in the family's home. He called his approach *theatre reciproque*. He found that the tragedies seemed much lighter, even funny, when repeated.

Moreno became a "miracle man" for some people, while some of the doctors claimed that he was not a real doctor because he was not using official papers to prescribe drugs and refused to put up an official doctor's plate outside his house. In response, Moreno placed a sign displaying his medical diploma at the entrance to his office (Marineau, 1989: 69).

He was warmly remembered in Vöslau. When he and his wife, Zerka, paid an unannounced visit to the city in 1959, 34 years after he had left, a crowd of older people gathered around him. He was recognized and greeted on the main square by an old lady in black. She came up to him, shook his hand and addressed him as: "*Unser Doktor*" (our doctor). The same warm recognition was his when he was honored in 1969 by the officials of Vöslau and a plaque was placed, in a charming ceremony, upon the house he had occupied during his tenure.

Spontaneity theater

A few years after the end of the First World War, when Austria was suffering from a lack of social and political leadership, Moreno thought of a plan that he hoped would bring all people together in a democratic way. On 1 April 1921, he hired the Komödienhaus in Vienna. When the curtain went up, Moreno was alone on the stage in the costume of a king's jester. On the stage were a throne, a crown, and a purple mantle. Moreno said that he was looking for a king, not one who crowns himself, but one whose wisdom makes him a natural choice for a leader. He then invited people to come up on the stage, talk about their ideas as leader, and to sit on the throne if they wished. Although his friends were supportive, many left the theater. As a production it was a disaster, although it was a demonstration of what Moreno came to call "sociodrama" as an action method dealing with intergroup relations and collective ideologies (Marineau, 1989: 71).

Sometime in 1922 Moreno rented space in Vienna with several rooms and a main hall that could hold between 50 and 75 people. Here a group of actors put on spontaneous plays in response to suggestions from the audience, and did re-enactments of the daily news in a "living newspaper," or improvised themes. After weeks of good reviews, the hall was often packed and the audience learned to become involved (Marineau, 1989: 72).

In 1922 Moreno had invented a three-tiered circular stage or action area where the protagonist in a psychodrama could present his or her world, reality, or life space. Moreno decided to present his stage design at an exhibition of new theater techniques in Vienna in 1924. An architect friend helped prepare sketches for the exhibition. However, the director of the exhibition actually built a somewhat similar circular stage. In this model, the audience sat in chairs that moved around the stage on a small railway. Moreno considered that there were too many similarities to his design, and at the opening of the exhibition publicly accused the director of plagiarism. This led to quite a stir in the press and to an appearance before a judge. In the courtroom, Moreno made a speech in which he said that his ideas were given anonymously and therefore belonged to the public. Thus, if someone claims public ideas for his own, "he has deprived the public of a good in a manner that violates moral law" (*Autobiography*, 1985, ch. 6: 39–45, cited in Marineau, 1989: 87).

Moreno recalled a night in 1925 that turned his spontaneity theater into a "therapeutic theater." An actress, Barbara, was part of his theater group and also took part in his new experiment with extemporaneous performance of events in the daily news (1972: 3–5). Barbara's specialty was playing roles of *ingénues* and heroic and romantic roles. One day her husband, George, came to Moreno to complain, "That sweet, angel-like being whom you admire, acts like a bedeviled creature when she is alone with me." Moreno asked the husband to attend the theater the next night. Barbara was now asked to play a role that would portray the rawness of human nature, its vulgarity and stupidity. Barbara was given the role of a streetwalker pursued by an actor playing the part of a man who attacked her. On stage she swore like a trooper, and punched and kicked the man. After the scene Barbara was exuberant with joy. She embraced George and they went home in ecstasy.

Moreno continued to give her roles of the same type and George gave daily reports. Barbara became less angry and George became more tolerant and less impatient with her. Moreno asked them if they would like to act together on the stage. Over a period of time, they portrayed scenes from her family and his, scenes from her childhood, and their dreams and plans for the future. Some months later, Moreno sat with them to analyze the development of their psychodrama, session by session, and to tell them the story of their progress. The sessions with Barbara and George illustrate the early use of psychodramatic techniques. In later years, Moreno referred to the sessions as psychodrama (1972: 5).

Moreno's early publications

Before the advent of the spontaneity theater, while still in Vienna, Moreno gathered around himself the literati and intelligentsia of his day. He never acquired a similar circle in the United States. He edited and published the magazine *Daimon*. The journal was published for five years and appeared under different names: in 1918 as *Daimon*, in 1919 as *Der Neue Daimon*, and from 1920 as *Die Gefahrten*.

The journal brought to public attention many new writers. Among them were Franz Werfel, Friedrich Schnack, Max Brod, Francis Jammes, Jakob Wassermann, Georg Kaiser, Martin Buber, Hugo Sonnenschein, Albert Ehrenstein, Ernst Block, Heinrich Mann, and Emil A. Rheinhardt. Moreno was mainly involved in founding the journal and in its first two years of publication. During that time he was directly and indirectly in touch with all the leading intellectuals of Vienna and Europe (Marineau, 1989: 56).

Moreno also wrote a novel, *Der Koenigsroman* (The king's novel, 1923b). His works in German were published anonymously. He believed that creativity was an anonymous category, the "name" was a form of capital never discovered by Marx. Since his works were not identifiable, this act of "casting his bread upon the waters" saved his work during a later period in Germany when the Nazis destroyed books written by Jews.

All of his papers during this period were published in German. The major themes can be seen in *Einladung zu einer Begegnung* (Invitation to an encounter, 1914–15) and *Das Stegreiftheater* (The theater of spontaneity, 1923a). The *Invitation to an Encounter* that was published in three parts represents Moreno's philosophy up to 1915. Several lines from a poem in the second part are often used to represent Moreno's basic idea of role reversal:

A meeting of two; eye to eye, face to face,
And when you are near I will tear your eyes out
and place them in place of mine,
and you will tear my eyes out
and will place them instead of yours,
then I will look at you with your eyes
and you will look at me with mine.

Moreno felt that he was creating a new positive religion that would take up the task of building a creative society where Karl Marx and Sigmund Freud had left off. He tried to do through sociometry what "religion without science" had failed to accomplish in the past and what "science without religion" had failed to accomplish in Soviet Russia.

Das Stegreiftheater was later translated as *The Theatre of Spontaneity* (1947c). In the book Moreno describes four kinds of revolutionary theater that are related: the theater of conflict, where the audience challenges the actors who are playing traditional roles; the theater of spontaneity, where everyone is part of the drama; therapeutic theater, as when members of a family re-enact a difficult situation; and the theater of the creator, which is everyone playing out life on the world's stage. The book also includes examples of Moreno's interaction diagrams depicting the amount of spontaneity in each act by each individual. However, we have found no record that Moreno ever used the system for research or in any further analysis of interaction.

Sociometry and psychodrama in the United States

Marineau (1989: 94–9) records that by 1925 Moreno found himself in a difficult situation. Although he had made some progress in establishing himself, he could never hope to be at ease and enjoy success in Austria. His relationship with Marianne had become difficult, and they were continually harassed by young anti-Semitic Vöslauers who would follow and threaten them. Moreno was practicing less as a doctor; the money he did earn went into his publishing ventures, and he was accumulating debts. The controversy over the design of the spontaneity theater did not help his reputation in the artistic and literary world. The suicide of a patient left him in some personal disarray; Moreno was becoming isolated.

Moreno considered emigrating to Russia where many of his friends had gone because of their political ideology. However, his brother William, who had already helped him a great deal financially, had already moved to New York. So Moreno decided to follow him, leaving Marianne in Bad Vöslau to take care of the house.

When Moreno left Vienna for the United States in 1925 it was to promote an electromagnetic recorder he had invented. The idea had occurred to him in a dream. It was a radio film to record sound on disks for radio transmission and reception. For the first two years in the United States (1925–7), he continued working on his invention with the help of Marianne's brother, Franz Lörnitzo, who was an engineering genius. However, there is no record of the invention being manufactured, although it is on record in the US patent office. Franz felt cheated and departed in anger. The family in Austria took sides with Franz, but Marianne remained faithful to Moreno.

Moreno then moved to New York where the early days were not easy. His letters to Marianne reveal depression and anger. He had hoped that his invention would be revolutionary and now he was without funds, although his brother William was supporting him. At one point he went to Canada to obtain a new temporary visa since he did not have a permanent visa for the United States and quotas made immigration difficult.

Before Moreno could practice medicine in New York State he needed a license. He sat for the examination for the first time in January 1927. The examination was in English and he was just starting to learn this new language. He failed the gynecology section, a subject he disliked, but took the examination again in May and was awarded his license in September 1927. By the end of 1927 Moreno's prospects had improved. He began private psychiatric practice and introduced psychodramatic work in several institutions.

Enter and exit Beatrice, exit Marianne

He met Beatrice Beecher, a social worker and a grand-daughter of Henry Ward Beecher, a famous evangelist in New York (Marineau, 1989: 96). Beatrice was lecturing on child psychology at Mount Sinai Hospital in New York. Moreno had given some demonstrations of spontaneity work with children at the hospital and Beatrice took an immediate interest in his work. She offered to marry him as a means of helping him obtain immigrant status on the assumption that they would obtain a divorce as soon as possible afterwards. They were married on 31 May 1928 and divorced in 1934 soon after Moreno became an American citizen. Moreno's relationship with Beatrice included professional cooperation. She worked on the first translation of *Das Stegreiftheater* and he gave demonstrations of work with children at the Plymouth Institute in Brooklyn where she was employed.

Moreno continued to correspond with Marianne and sent money to pay off some of his debts. Marianne kept the house in Bad Vöslau unaware of Moreno's marriage to Beatrice Beecher and his meetings with other younger women. When in 1930 Marianne could no longer keep the city council from taking over their house, Moreno became very upset and used the opportunity to break off the relationship with Marianne. Much later, Marianne married. She died in 1984, leaving behind her correspondence with Moreno as a record of her involvement with the man and his dream.

Impromptu theater, Helen Jennings and sociometry

In 1927, Moreno had organized a new version of the spontaneity theater, the "impromptu theater." Performances of the "living newspaper" were given at Carnegie Hall (1929–31), where the news events of the day were acted out. He was also training well-established actors and actresses in new methods.

It was at the impromptu theater that Moreno met Helen H. Jennings, then a graduate student at Columbia University. She in turn introduced Moreno to Professor Gardner Murphy, who became a supporter and associate and provided a connection between Moreno and social psychologists and sociologists. Helen Jennings became the driving force behind the development of sociometry, leading to the work at Sing Sing prison, the Hudson School for Girls, and other research. Although Moreno was very close to Helen and considered her a talented social scientist, he apparently did not wish to become emotionally involved with her.

The next 20 years were the most productive in Moreno's life. His brother, William, continued to support him with both time and money, and in 1941–2 helped to establish the Sociometric Institute in New York. Moreno records that during this period William was his muse, the only member of his family who ever gave him full support and encouragement. However, about this time Moreno went through a period of wildness. He began to meditate on how rapidly life vanishes. He recalls: "Moments of great joy vanish as rapidly as moments of profound disgust. Actresses, chorus girls, writers, psychologists, rebels; many tried to seduce me. Many succeeded" (1989b: 106).

Moreno's ideas about spontaneity and creativity were published in the magazine *Impromptu* which Moreno produced and published in 1931, and later reprinted in the first volume of *Psychodrama* (1972, first edition 1946).

His work in sociometry at Sing Sing prison led to monographs on the group method for the classification of prisoners, collected in *The First Book on Group Psychotherapy: 1932* (1957b). The results of his research, with the help of Helen Jennings, on the individual relationships within a group of prisoners, were presented at a round table conference at the Annual Meeting of the American Psychiatric Association in 1932, marking the formal start of Moreno's contribution to group psychotherapy.[3]

He became involved in yet another controversy. At the meetings, Dr Abraham A. Brill presented a paper on "Lincoln as a humorist." Moreno was asked to act as a discussant. Moreno not only attacked the content of the paper on the grounds that one could not interpret the personality of a dead person, but also was critical of Brill himself. His statement brought him immediate notoriety since an account of the event appeared in American and international papers the next day. Many psychoanalysts turned against Moreno.

Moreno's confrontations with psychoanalysis continued throughout his career, especially with S. R. Slavson, the proponent of psychoanalytic group therapy in the United States. Both men created separate organizations and journals and competed for national and world leadership in their fields. Berger (1990) gives more details of the controversy between the two men and also comments on other aspects of Moreno's biography.

Mrs Fannie French Morse, superintendent of the New York State Training School for Girls in Hudson, attended Moreno's presentation at the American Psychiatric Association meeting. The impression he made led to his appointment as the Director of Research at the school for 1932–4. At Hudson, Moreno made 16 mm films to illustrate group psychotherapy and role training, both new methods of training. The results of the sociometric research at Hudson were presented in 1934 in *Who Shall Survive?*. The book was dedicated to Mrs Morse in recognition of her support. A foreword by Dr William A. White pays tribute to Moreno's philosophy. Some of the results of the study were also published in 1936 as a report to the directors in the *Sociometric Review*. In a revision and expansion of this book, published in 1953, Moreno added a discussion of all of the important concepts in psychodrama, sociodrama, and sociatry. This was his *magnum opus*.

In 1933 Moreno met Howard Blakeslee, a journalist from the Associated Press. Through this contact, he published articles about sociometry and psychodrama in newspapers that reached a wide audience. Blakeslee convinced Moreno that he should try to predict the winner of the forthcoming heavyweight boxing match between Max Baer and Joe Louis. Moreno visited each boxer's camp, observed their spontaneity and their relationships to family and friends. Moreno even published a chart showing the positive and negative influences in Baer's life. Moreno successfully predicted Lewis's win and Moreno repeated the exercise for two other fights.

In 1937 Moreno began to publish the journal *Sociometry: a Journal of Inter-Personal Relations*. This brought into his orbit sociologists and social psychologists, besides psychiatrists and clinical psychologists. The authors of the articles in the early editions of *Sociometry* include many of his followers, notable among them were George Lundberg and Charles Loomis. In 1941 Dr White, superintendent at St Elizabeth's Hospital in Washington, DC, made it possible for Moreno to construct a psychodrama theater in the hospital.

The psychodrama theater and Florence Bridge as temporary muse

Moreno continued to search for a muse (Marineau, 1989: 101–7). He met Florence Bridge who was doing an internship at the Hudson School. She was born in 1912 and was 23 years younger than Moreno.[4] She was very impressed with Moreno as a prophet, especially in his book *The Words of the Father*. The theme of God was a major bond in their relationship. Moreno was then living by himself on the property of the sanatorium that he had opened in Beacon, New York in 1936. With funds supplied by a wealthy patient, he had built his first psychodrama theater next to the hospital. After Florence moved to Beacon, they were married in 1938 and had a daughter, Regina, the following year.

Although Florence admired Moreno and treated him almost as a God, the marriage was not a happy one for him. He was still looking for someone like Marianne who could be a professional partner and co-creator. Florence had little contact with the patients at the sanatorium. She lived in the little house on the property, looking after her daughter. Even though she contributed some professional articles in the field of sociometry, she never captured the imagination of her husband. They were married for ten stormy years. Meanwhile, Moreno had found his real muse and found himself in a difficult situation. Florence and Moreno were divorced in 1948.

Enter Zerka as ultimate muse

In 1941 Celine Zerka Toeman had visited Moreno's office at the Beacon sanatorium when she brought her psychotic sister for treatment. Moreno felt that it was "love at first sight." Zerka was a fashion designer and had never thought of becoming involved in the field of psychology; however, she soon joined in his projects. He asked her to read proofs of the English translation of *The Words of the Father*. Her immediate understanding of the book and his philosophy cemented the relationship. She became his constant associate and companion. Moreno asked her to take charge of his office in New York City for the Institute of Sociometry. It was also the office of the Theater of Psychodrama for which his brother, William, had provided the financial backing and was taking care of daily operations. Zerka soon became a partner in the project. At the sanatorium, she became Moreno's inspiration, co-therapist, co-researcher, and his true love. From 1942, when Zerka and Moreno published their first article, "The group approach in psychodrama" (Moreno and Toeman, 1942), Zerka was his partner giving him support, in his publications, conferences, workshops, and other ventures. Marineau (1989: 105) notes that "Moreno did not completely avoid other women after he met Zerka, but nobody was a threat to her, for nobody contributed as much to the development of Moreno's ideas as she did."[5]

Moreno married Zerka in 1949. They had a son, Jonathan, in 1952. Moreno provided part of Jonathan's education using psychodramatic techniques. He and Zerka would use role reversal to give all three members of the family a better understanding of each other's needs and feelings. Many articles and a book were published that were based on his experience of child-rearing and family development. Zerka developed a chondrosarcoma in her shoulder, and in 1958 had to have her right arm amputated. Again the family used psychodramatic techniques to explore thoughts and feelings and to support each other.

Moreno was also active in promoting group psychotherapy. In 1945 he edited a special combined issue of *Sociometry* on the subject, published under the title: *Group Psychotherapy: a Symposium*. This volume includes a paper reporting the use of group methods in the British army during the Second World War. One of the more anonymous distinctions that Moreno received that pleased him enormously was conveyed by Dr J. R. Rees, then head of the World Mental Health Organization. Rees told Moreno that after a representative of the British military had studied with Moreno in 1943, a special organization within the British army was formed to develop group methods of selection. The organization was informally designated as "The Moreno Brigade."

Although his sociometric methods received widespread acceptance, Zerka notes that Moreno was a problem for the psychiatric fraternity: "His views of man, and his interpersonal and intergroup relations flew in the face of all that was being taught. He was just too controversial, too personally difficult to accept: a maverick, a loner, a narcissistic leader, charismatic but aloof, gregarious but selective, lovable but eccentric, unlovable and appealing" (1976: 132).

He developed more long-lasting relationships outside the world of psychiatry than within it, although he had friendly relations with many. One of the earlier friends was Alfred Adler, who referred a number of patients to him with the recommendation: "If I could do what he does, I would call myself a genius."

Promoting group psychotherapy

During the 18 years from 1936 to 1953, Moreno wrote mainly on the major concepts and methods of sociometry and psychodrama. In 1936 he had opened his sanatorium at Beacon, New York, and in 1942 he founded the Theatre of Psychodrama, Psychodramatic Institute, and Sociometric Institute in New York City. He was a special lecturer at the New School for Social Research in 1937–8, and at Teachers College, Columbia University, in 1939–40. In 1931, he began to publish *Impromptu*, a journal concerned with dramatics and therapy; in 1937, he founded the journal *Sociometry*; *Sociatry* was founded in 1947, but changed to *Group Psychotherapy* in 1949, and *Group Psychotherapy and Psychodrama* in 1970. From 1951 through 1966 he was an adjunct professor in the Department of Sociology in the Graduate School of Arts and Sciences at New York University. His students at New York University included Edgar Borgatta, Lewis Yablonsky, Martin Haskell, Hannah Weiner, Robert Boguslaw, and Robert Siroka. Early followers who studied at the psychodrama institutes at Beacon or in New York City included psychologists and educators: James Enneis, Robert Haas, Paul Torrance, and Ron Levy. Another educator greatly influenced by Moreno was Merl E. Bonney. In addition, some of the social psychologists who founded the National Training Laboratories for Group Dynamics, Ronald Lippitt, Alvin Zander, Kenneth Benne, and Lee Bradford, were influenced by Moreno and used role playing in their work.

In 1951 he organized the International Committee on Group Psychotherapy, later enlarged and renamed the International

Council of Group Psychotherapy, which became responsible for arranging and sponsoring a series of international congresses on group psychotherapy. The first one took place in 1954 in Toronto. He was elected president of the Second International Congress of Group Psychotherapy, 1957, the International Council of Group Psychotherapy, 1962, and the Third International Congress of Group Psychotherapy, 1963. In 1961 he had created the World Academy of Psychodrama and Group Psychotherapy of which he was the first president. The first International Congress of Psychodrama was held in Paris in 1964. After this first congress, psychodramatists met regularly for international meetings in Latin America, Europe, and Japan. Moreno was Honorary President of the International Congress of Psychodrama and Sociodrama. Before his death he was able to transform the council into an incorporated International Association of Group Psychotherapy numbering almost 800 members from many countries. This was his last achievement; it took place during the fifth international congress in Zurich in August 1973.

Twenty-six years after he had departed from Europe, Moreno began a series of trips to bring group psychotherapy and other areas of his concern to the attention of his overseas colleagues. The Sorbonne honored him with the establishment of a Sociometric Institute in the Sociology Department, then under the guidance of Georges Gurvitch. In 1954, he was invited by the US State Department to undertake a tour of various universities and America Houses in West Germany. Similar tours were later undertaken at regular intervals throughout Europe; several included invitations by the United Nations Educational, Scientific and Cultural Organization. The countries, some of which were visited repeatedly, were France, Germany, Norway, Switzerland, Austria, Italy, Spain, Czechoslovakia, Hungary, Russia, Greece, (the former) Yugoslavia, Turkey, and Israel.

The third psychiatric revolution

During the seven years from 1954 to 1960, Moreno traveled extensively and saw the spread of his ideas in the social science literature throughout the world. "The third psychiatric revolution," as he termed it, had now arrived. The group had become both doctor and patient. Moreno's articles on psychodrama were in wide demand for collections of readings and handbooks. From 1956 through 1960 he edited five volumes of *Progress in Psychotherapy*, first with Frieda Fromm-Reichmann as senior editor and then with Jules H. Masserman. He also published *Gruppenpsychotherapie und Psychodrama* (1959a), which is similar to the third volume of *Psychodrama* (1969), written in collaboration with Zerka, but also contains original material that was never translated into English.

Review and evaluation

The last period, from 1961 until his death on 14 May 1974, was one in which Moreno reviewed the history of the movements he had initiated and evaluated their impact. Additional articles appeared in collections, handbooks, and foreign publications, as his work continued to be recognized.

Moreno does not give much space in his writing to acknowledgment of the people whose work influenced his own creativity. He was much more concerned about how his ideas were being used by others, often he thought without due credit. As a social reformer, he saw himself in the tradition of Jean Jacques Rousseau, Johann H. Pestalozzi, and Friedrich Froebel, although he wished to keep the initiative for reform in the hands of the people.

The Medical Society of the State of New York, of which he was a life member, gave him a citation in 1967 in recognition of 50 years of medical practice. He closed his hospital at Beacon in that year and continued only with training and publishing. As Moreno became less able to carry out a demanding schedule, Zerka became more prominent in the training program. In the late 1960s and early 1970s, she took over the leadership to become an established figure in group psychotherapy and psychodrama. Beacon continued as a training center after Moreno's death until 1982 when the former hospital, then the Moreno Institute, was sold. In 1968 Moreno received an honorary doctorate from the Medical Faculty of the University of Barcelona (Spain), and in 1969 a Golden Doctor Diploma from the University of Vienna. In the same year a plaque was placed on the house in Vöslau near Vienna to commemorate his work there as a public health officer from 1918 to 1925.

He was a fellow of the American Psychiatric Association, a member of the New York Medical Society and the American Sociological Association, a life member of the American Medical Association, and a member of the American Society for Group Psychotherapy and Psychodrama, and the American Sociometric Association, of which he was president in 1945.

Moreno seemed to feel most expansive when he thought of himself as a sociologist who had initiated the new scientific sociology in the form of sociometry. In 1953, he packed all of his best ideas into his revision of *Who Shall Survive?* Moreno recalls a small meeting room at Columbia University where a few people were sitting, musing about where sociometry would lead (1953: lxvi–lxvii).

One of the younger scholars took me aside and said bluntly: "You seem to think that *Who Shall Survive?* is a book of books, a new bible." I looked at him and saw the green light of "creator envy" in his eye. Of course I thought so, but I did not say a word. I smiled at him and he smiled back. It is a new bible, the bible for social conduct, for human societies. It has more ideas packed in one book than a whole generation of books. What is wrong with a bible? Some people have an idea that a bible stops everything. On the contrary, in the religious sphere the Old and New Testaments did not stop religion, they opened new vistas and stimulated religious experience and techniques. The same thing happened in science. *The fear of bibles is the fear of anything which is definite and decisive.*

Notes

1 The sources for all the material in this chapter are Zerka Moreno (1976), Hare (1979, 1986b), Marineau (1989), and Moreno's autobiography (1989); see also Toeman (1949). However, in order not to break up the text with line by line citations, references are only given for material that is a direct quotation, or, although not quoted directly, presents information or an opinion about Moreno where the source is important. For additional comments on Moreno's life, see Zerka Moreno (1969a), Nolte (1989) and Cramer-Azima (1990).

2 In a letter dated 20 June 1995, Zerka Moreno tells us that "I have some trouble reconciling this with the fact that I have photos of him taken during the First World War in uniform with some other medical colleagues equally uniformed and another one where he is in a surgical tent, obviously in the field (he told me it was Hungary), administering anesthesia to a patient. I also, years later, found an Austrian passport among his papers with which he came to this country [the United States]; having served in the military would make him eligible for that hard-to-obtain citizenship. I take this story of his to be related to [the story of] having been born on a ship on the Black Sea when Marineau found every evidence of his birth in Bucharest, one of his homespun myths."

3 Moreno had used the term "group psychotherapy" in an address at the meeting of the American Psychiatric Association in 1932. He cites an unpublished paper by Renouvier to bolster his claim to have initiated group psychotherapy (Moreno, 1953: lvi). Renouvier argues that, although other therapists before Moreno were aware that the group had some influence on the individual, they did not have a method of measurement which sociometry provided, and thus could not be aware of the full meaning of the term "group" in "group psychotherapy." However, we note that the term "group psychotherapy" in contemporary usage refers to a therapist conducting therapy with a group of patients. Moreno's work in the Sing Sing prison involved the classification of prisoners according to salient social characteristics and organizing groups of prisoners around a prisoner leader. This presumably improved the functioning and control of the prisoners, but there is no indication that therapists were directly involved in group therapy (Moreno, 1957b).

4 Zerka Moreno's record (letter dated 20 June 1995) of several facts concerning Florence Bridge differs from that of Marineau. Whereas Marineau says that Florence was "almost twenty-five years younger than Moreno," Zerka notes that Florence was born in 1912 and Moreno in 1889, a difference of twenty-three years. Zerka adds that Florence was not trained as a social worker but did help with research at the Hudson School under Helen Jennings's guidance, and therefore did not meet Moreno while he was demonstrating sociometry at Columbia University according to Marineau's account. Zerka writes "when J.L. opened the Sanitarium at Beacon he needed an aide and Helen Jennings suggested Florence who was in need of a job; this was the depression era and she only had a BA then. When she came, Mrs Gertrude Franchot Tone [a wealthy patient in Moreno's sanitarium who gave money to build the theater at Beacon] was envious of her youth and beauty and Moreno sent her to study at Columbia where she received her masters at Teachers College in Early Childhood Education and in fact became a kindergarten teacher after they were divorced, at least for a while before she married again."

5 In a letter, dated 20 June 1995, Zerka Moreno records: "At the time I met J.L. I was working as a private secretary to a Dutch Importer to whom I was useful because of being multi-lingual and I conducted his correspondence in Dutch, French, German and English. The fact that I was a good typist and always wanted to work on manuscripts with a creative writer was an extra attraction. I was useful from the start and earned my scholarship with J.L. by immediately working with him. In fact, I set up his filing system; he used to keep his correspondence in a large laundry basket on the floor of his office behind his chair at the desk. I changed all that as well as overhauling the entire filing system in his office, including that of patients' records."

2
Major Contributions to Theory

Just as Moreno's life covered a wide range of activities, from theater to therapy, from numerical analysis of interpersonal relationships to the experience of direct encounters with God, both his theoretical contributions and his practice cover a similar range. The major themes in his life are reflected in the theoretical contributions, his research, and his form of therapy.

Moreno tells us that his life began as a wanderer. His experience as an immigrant probably sensitized him to the problems of the newcomer, of finding support in a new community to be creative. He noted that as an individual moves from an old to a new community, the network of social relationships changes its membership, but the constellation tends to be constant (1953: 705). His concern for the immigrant is evident in the House of Encounter, established while a student in Vienna, as an absorption center for new immigrants, in his observations at the refugee camp at Mitterndorf, and later at Hudson School, where the focus was on the placement of a new girl in a house.

Moreno's God-playing and direct experiences with the creator has assured him that the central focus of human interaction was creativity. His experience with his muses gave evidence that, with proper support, each individual could take a place in the creative process and be part of the cosmic plan, to provide continuing creativity, if not for the whole society, at least for the "moment" since existentially the encounter was all that was experienced.

Had Moreno been a director of a traditional theater, he might have introduced "drama therapy" where individuals can gain a new sense of self by playing roles in a set drama. However, he was a director of spontaneous theater and thus had the opportunity to observe the process of "warm up" for creative enactment and also the possibility of using spontaneous role playing to recreate scenes from an individual's past life, to gain catharsis and new insights. Thus, spontaneous theater became a source of concepts for understanding interpersonal relations as well as a method of group therapy.

At the time Moreno was writing, the ideal model of science was represented by physics, chemistry, and biology. Moreno borrowed many concepts from these sciences as metaphors for ideas about interpersonal choice and other aspects of interpersonal behavior. By his own account, Moreno's ambition was to construct:

1 a *personality theory* which is superior to that of Freud – psycho-drama,
2 a *social theory* which is superior to that of Marx – sociometry, and
3 a *cosmic theory* which is superior to that of the Old and New Testament, the Koran and the Speeches of Buddha – The Words of the Father . . . (Bischof, 1970: 235n)

Moreno referred to the largest system that he had constructed as *socionomy*, the science of social laws. It has three branches: *socio-dynamics*, the science of the structure of social aggregates; *sociometry*, the science of social measurement (although its main focus was the measurement of interpersonal choice); and *sociatry*, the science of social healing (Moreno et al., 1960: 127). The proper focus of social science for Moreno was "action" rather than "behavior." "Action" refers to the living existence of movements and facts, whereas "behavior" refers to the observation of the movements and facts. A real action system must deal with spontaneity, creativity, and warming up. Observers must become actors to have a sense of the consensus necessary for an actorial system (Moreno et al., 1960: 130). Moreno felt compelled to develop a psychology of the creative act, to recognize the limitations of humans as spontaneous creative agents and to invent spontaneity techniques which might lift them beyond these limitations (1953: 8).

Moreno's theoretical concepts

Although Moreno could be very formal in his statements of theory, with extensive sets of hypotheses for further testing, he also left behind pages of insights about social life scattered through short notes published in one of his journals or in dialogues with colleagues published as "proceedings" or presented as responses to comments on lectures he had given. We leave the task of bringing together all of Moreno's insights in one coherent picture for some future time, probably by some future authors. Here, we present a summary of the main and most often quoted of his theoretical statements.[1]

Elaborations of Moreno's theoretical ideas will continue to appear throughout this text. In Chapter 3, some of the concepts and relationships come to life in the descriptions of psychodramas that Moreno conducted and in his application of sociometry at the Hudson School for Girls. In Chapter 4, in a series of "lectures," Moreno amplifies his ideas related to group psychotherapy. Comments by his contemporaries in Chapter 5 place Moreno's ideas in the general context of social-psychological theory. A few terms, such as "tele," which were so central for Moreno, will appear over and over again.

Central to Moreno's theory are the concepts of spontaneity and creativity in society and in the individual. He begins by emphasizing a feature of existence which most social scientists leave out: his perception of the role of God as the creator of the universe who placed human beings on Earth to continue to be creative in adapting to changes in their environmental, physical, and social situation.

Within societies, communities, organizations, and small groups, Moreno was most interested in the networks of interpersonal choice, the "social atoms," that related to each individual, which through "encounter" could enhance creativity. The creativity that Moreno felt was the essence of life was that which occurred at "the moment" when there was a sense that the interaction had achieved a new understanding of the relationship between the self and the other.

It would seem that, based on his experience as a student in establishing a house for transients in Vienna, and with displaced persons at Mitterndorf, he had concluded that individual creativity and indeed the "creative revolution" could take place if societal structures, especially those reflecting interpersonal choice, could be rearranged to provide maximum support for the creativity of each individual. At the level of personality, he proposed a theory and practice for child development that would result in a "spontaneous person."

From the top down, for communities, organizations, and groups, he sought to rearrange the networks of choice to promote maximum creativity. From the bottom up, for the individual, he introduced psychodrama both for "social atom repair work" and to help people move beyond emotions and perceptions that might be blocking their creativity. To the extent that all group activity has an undercurrent of "social drama," the progression through the phases of a psychodrama is also a theory of group development and change. Moreno's "sociodrama" also provides a model of the phases in social change for communities and societies.

As we have noted, many of Moreno's basic concepts can be traced back to his early childhood or the years in Vienna as a medical student and later as a young doctor. He made many of the connections in the stories he told in the preface to the 1953 edition of *Who Shall Survive?* and in his autobiography (1989a, b). Zerka Moreno (1969b) indicates the source of concepts such as "encounter" and "group therapy" in Moreno's early written work.

Here, we present Moreno's theoretical ideas in approximate chronological order of the years in which he was most active using them. First, his ideas about God and their implications for human behavior from his years in Austria. Next, after moving to the United States, his applications of social measurement and social reorganization at the Hudson School for Girls. Next, his concepts concerning aspects of interpersonal behavior in small groups and larger social systems. This section includes his ideas about relationships that occur primarily in the dyad (tele, encounter, and co-unconscious) as well as forms of interaction that can take place in the dyad and also in larger groups (creativity, role enactment). Finally, his ideas about child development based on his research with Florence Moreno and his collaboration, with Zerka, in helping their son, Jonathan, to become a spontaneous person. Examples of their interventions are given in *Psychodrama, Second Volume* (Moreno and Moreno, 1959: 135–87) and *The First Psychodramatic Family* (Moreno et al., 1964). If all children had the opportunity for an experience of spontaneity and creativity, they would become creative adults, as the co-creators with God. There would be no need for "sociatrists" to intervene to diagnose and treat sick societies nor for psychodramatists to direct individuals in their social reconstruction. As Moreno had recorded in *The Words of the Father* (1971: 137) "all men are born to create" and thus should be able to go about their business without further assistance.

God and the individual as co-creators in the cosmos

For most of his professional life in the United States, Moreno did not draw attention to *The Words of the Father* and his own direct contact with the creativity of God, since this would not have been in keeping with the contemporary "scientific" approach to the study of social behavior. In 1969, Moreno noted that:

> very early in my career I came to the position that there is another area, a larger world beyond the psychodynamics and sociodynamics of human society – *cosmodynamics*. Man is a *cosmic man*, not only a social man or an individual man. When I first said this, about fifty years ago, it sounded a little bit like highly exaggerated mysticism. Today it is almost common sense. Man is a cosmic being. (Moreno and Moreno, 1969: 19)

The cosmos is considered by Moreno to be the fourth universal phenomenon, the first three being time (past, present, and future), space (the environment in which action takes place), and reality. Psychodrama provided a therapeutic setting where each of these dimensions could be explored, with the possibility of introducing *surplus reality* by representing intangible and invisible dimensions of intrapsychic and extrapsychic life. For Moreno, any therapeutic method that did not concern itself with the cosmic implications of action, with the destiny of human beings, would be incomplete and inadequate.

The inherent creativity of God and humanity means that just as all things are changing they can be further changed. On the psychodrama stage the protagonist can have the experience of changing sex, age, or any other personal or interpersonal aspect of the situation to provide some insight into the possibilities for change in the "real" world. For Moreno,

> the psychodramatic answer to the claim that God is dead is that he can be easily restored to life. Following the example of Christ, we have given him and can give him new life, but not in the form our ancestors cherished. We have replaced the dead God by millions of people who can embody God in their own person. (Moreno and Moreno, 1969: 21)

Their destiny is to continue the process of creativity, especially in interpersonal relations.

Blatner underscores Moreno's hope that people would come to think of themselves as co-creators of a greater dynamic wholeness (Blatner and Blatner, 1988: 56). Blatner saw Moreno as more of a visionary than a systematic philosopher and more of a poet than a theoretician: one who wrote with inspired devotion about his vision of people recognizing the divine nature within themselves.

Networks of interpersonal relations

Moreno's theory of society focused on the networks of interpersonal relations that join individuals. The networks can be visualized in "sociograms" showing choices and rejections given and received between the members of a society, community, organization, or group. The psychogeographic mapping of a community reveals underlying "networks" (Moreno et al., 1960: 67). Moreno gives as an example of networks those of girls who had run away from the Hudson School. To test the network, Moreno planted a rumor to see how it would travel. He concluded that one can control networks if they are reached when the ideas are only simmering. Further, individuals and families can be assigned places in communities where neighbors will be mutually attracted and mutually beneficial. The architect of the future will be a student of social geometry.

Moreno offers several hypotheses related to the distribution of individuals in networks. If a group has several networks that are not connected, it is "polarized." Groups with high polarity will have more conflicts. The formation of networks between individuals is subject to the *Law of social gravitation*: people in two different locations will move towards each other in proportion to attraction, inversely with rejection, and the amount of distance between locations. There is also a *Sociodynamic law* (effect): some people receive most of the choices and some are persistently left out. As group size is increased, an even greater proportion of choices go to those at the top (1953: 698). The distribution is different from that resulting from chance. In addition, there are more complex structures (triangles, squares, chains) in the actual sociograms. One should count the number of structures as well as the number of choices received by each individual as an indication of the characteristics of the collective. There may be some minimum number of chains and other networks for a society to function (Moreno et al., 1960: 30–9). *Tele* (a form of two-way empathy) and emotional and social expansiveness develop with age. However, cleavages based on age, sex, or ethnic group also become apparent (1953: 699).[2]

The higher the social status of an individual, the more frequent the interaction with other members of the group, and more frequently will the individual be allowed to initiate action in a situation (1953: 703). The sociometric status of an individual rises when connected by *tele* with an individual of higher status (1953: 704). Extreme extroverted or introverted groups (choices outside or inside) are low on stability and cohesion (1953: 705). Individuals with larger acquaintance volumes also have larger social atoms. *Social entropy* is a sociodynamic decline in choices, the cooling off of emotional expansiveness. When interest in others has reached a climax, the introduction of new members into a community will not lead to new choices. At this time the collective spontaneity has reached zero. Ambivalence may result if a person is chosen on one criterion and rejected on another (1953: 708). The structure of the group is related to the task. For some tasks, pairs may be the ideal sets of relationships (1953: 712). Physical proximity plays a part since, following a principle of least effort, it is easier to know people who are close to you (1953: 716).

A predominantly psycho-organic level of society, with more physical intimacy, must have preceded the present psychosocial level. This change was accompanied by increased individualism and differentiation of groups to form more complex patterns according to a *sociogenetic law*. To answer the question "who shall survive?," one must first ask "are there social laws of natural selection?" The answer is yes, natural selection takes place in small groups where some individuals are pushed out of the network. In the ideal society, no one is cast out (Moreno et al., 1960: 6). All are given an opportunity to participate to the best of their abilities to survive. As Moreno continued to affirm, he sought a "technique of freedom; to balance the spontaneous forces for the greatest harmony and unity of all" (Moreno, 1934: 7; Moreno et al., 1960: 7).

The social atom

The set of people who form the relationships that are the most significant for each individual Moreno designated as the *social atom*. As Moreno defines it: "The social atom is the nucleus of all individuals towards whom a person is related in a significant manner or who are related to him at the same time; the relationship may be emotional, social, or cultural." It is indicated by "the sum of the interpersonal structures resulting from choices and rejections centered about a given individual. . .". Attractions and repulsions are not emotions but their end products (Moreno et al., 1960: 52). Moreno asserts that the social atom is the smallest social unit, unlike the physical atom which has smaller structures within it (electrons, neutrons, etc.).[3]

The number of acquaintances at a given time is the *acquaintance volume*. The social atom is the core. The social atom can be divided into a central core of actual relationships and an outer core of wished-for relationships (Moreno et al., 1960: 55). An individual can also be asked about preferences for things, objects, values and objectives; for example, sex, food, money, or ideas. A person who places a high value on money will choose others who share the same value. Moreno suggests adding the value inventory as a measure of the "character" of an individual. "It is probable that there will be found a close relationship between the tendency to have a strong affinity for persons and the tendency to have a weak affinity for things; and vice versa" (Moreno et al., 1960: 58).

Some people may be attracted to others possessing certain characteristics, a general category, rather than to specific individuals. However, attraction to a particular individual may break through attraction to a general category. "A monk, subscribing to a certain idea of conduct, may act toward everyone he meets with the same 'equalized' affection until this attitude is suddenly interrupted by an individual to whom he is sensitive."

Moreno suggests three options for the future. Society might become one in which there are only feelings for things, not people. The emotional currents between persons would be reduced to zero. Examples are the "solitaire," the saint, and the schizophrenic. Or there might be a society in which there are only attachments to people (no examples are given) or there might be no attachment to either things or people, for example a society of Buddhas (Moreno et al., 1960: 60–1). (Moreno does not state a preference.)

"As we grow older replacements of lost members in significant roles take place with greater difficulty . . . a social death. Old people should try to restore the youth of their social atom. The life of a person extends beyond death through the social atom" (Moreno et al., 1960: 63–4). For individuals to continue to be creative they must be surrounded by supportive social atoms and networks.

Sociometric criteria

The criterion that forms the basis for interpersonal choice, whether the other person is chosen for a "task" or "social" reason, is very important for understanding society. The size of the human population approximates two and a half billion individuals, but the number of inter-individual associations existing on the Earth is many times larger because, in a sociometric sense, every person belongs to many more small groups than are visible at one time. Millions of small groups are continually formed and dissolved. It is the "criterion" that gives every sociometrically defined small group its momentum, the common motive which draws individuals together spontaneously for a certain end. The criterion may be as fundamental as a search for home and shelter, as a need for food and sleep, as for love and companionship, or as casual as a game of cards.

There are millions of criteria on which groupings are continually forming. They give overt and tangible human society a deeply unconscious and complicated "infra" structure. It is difficult to uncover because of its remoteness from immediate experience and because there is no strict separation between the "infra" and the overt structures. One is interwoven with the other. At times, genuine interpersonal structures can be perceived on the surface; at other times, they require extensive sociomicroscopic study before they can be discovered (1953: 96–7).

Choice, motivation, and cause

For his theory of interpersonal choice, Moreno provided a form of measurement, the sociometric test. Sociometric testing is carried out in three phases:

1　Spontaneous choice.
2　Motivation of these choices.
3　Causation of these choices.

Spontaneous choice reveals how many members of an individual's own group, whatever the criterion that brought the group members together, are desired by an individual as associates in an activity of this group. The motivations, as they are secured through an interview with each individual, reveal further the number of attractions and repulsions to which an individual is exposed in a group activity. The underlying causes of these attractions and repulsions are studied through spontaneity and role playing tests adapted to sociometric aims.

The spontaneity test places an individual in a standard life situation which calls for definite fundamental emotional reactions, called spontaneity states, such as fear or anger. If permitted to expand, they turn into role playing. The range of mimic and verbal expression during the role plays is recorded and offers characteristic clues to the make-up of the personality of the actor, to the individual's relations to the life situation acted, and to the person or persons who act opposite in the test. Examples of the use of the various tests are given in Chapter 3 in the summary of Moreno's work at the Hudson School for Girls.

Tele is responsible for mutual choice. If there are two reciprocal first choices in a pair, then there is more *tele* than, say, a first choice and a third choice.[4] Moreno provides charts depicting different forms of *tele*: simple, symbolic, object, "infra" and others. However, these remain as hypotheses since Moreno never had an opportunity to demonstrate the differences between the types through research or any systematic observation. He orders some of the concepts by "degrees of intensity." He proposes scores for groups, comparing the number of choices given to persons inside the group with the number given to persons outside the group (Moreno et al., 1960: 39–42).

Moreno refers to the most elementary social relationships, including the social and cultural atoms and networks of communication, as the "sociometric universalia." They are found in all societies independent of cultural context. These are the social facts that are present in the social system to be revealed by social science

(1953: 617–18). A detailed summary appears in *Who Shall Survive?* (1953: 696–717) under the heading "General hypotheses and recommendations for further research." The summary takes the form of a list of 107 hypotheses and generalizations to be found in the various "books" that make up the single volume of *Who Shall Survive?* This list of hypotheses provides part of the basis for the present chapter.[5]

After completing his research at the Hudson School for Girls in the 1930s, Moreno was not directly involved in sociometric research, although he continued to publish articles drawing on data from this period. He kept abreast of current sociometric research conducted by others that was published in his journal and monograph series.[6]

The cornerstone of sociometry is the "doctrine of spontaneity and creativity" (Moreno et al., 1960: x). The method of data collection used in true sociometric research involves warming subjects up to give valid data: "a social science becomes sociometric to the degree in which it gives the members of the group research status" by making them participating and evaluating actors. "Sociometry is recognized by what it does, stirring to action and keeping action open but using scientific precision and experimental methods to keep action in bounds" (Moreno et al., 1960: xii).

If judged by these criteria of Moreno's, little past or current research would be classified as "sociometric" since subjects are rarely asked to perform an action based on their understanding of interpersonal relationships that results from having participated in a sociometric test situation. Thus, even if Moreno had chosen to expand his action theory by building on the results of the many studies of interpersonal choice, he would have had little useful data for the analysis of the effects of becoming spontaneous and creative. His best evidence was from the studies of the effects of participation in psychodramas (covered in Chapter 3) but even then, when the psychodrama directors were using an action method, there was little follow-up to validate the effects of the participation. However, as Moreno claimed, the main validation may have been "existential."

Three dimensions of society

There are three dimensions of society: the external reality, the sociometric matrix, and the social reality. The external reality consists of the tangible and visible groupings, both legitimate (family, church) and illegitimate (gangs, crowds). The sociometric matrix consists of the relationships, revealed by sociometry, that are otherwise invisible. The social reality is a dynamic synthesis of external reality and the sociometric matrix. Social conflict increases in proportion to sociodynamic difference between official society and the sociometric matrix.[7] The scientist is an action agent with the subjects as co-actors. The laboratory becomes life itself. The nearer the sociometric procedure to the life frame, the more adequate are the data collected. We must understand the warming up process of moving individuals and groups into action. Choices should reflect decisions for action, not attitudes (Moreno et al., 1960: 118–26). Social aggregates result from a combination of choices based on biological, economic, religious, and cultural factors.

Tele, encounter, and co-unconscious

As noted, *tele* is defined as: insight into, appreciation of, and feeling for the actual make-up of another person (Moreno et al., 1960: 17). This is what happens during an encounter. Social configurations consist of two or multiple ways of interaction. *Tele* includes both empathy and transference. The greater the social distance between individuals, the more inaccurate will be the perceptions of their relationship.

The principle of encounter: Two individuals meet face to face and experience each other as actors. There is total reciprocity. The encounter happens in *the moment*, in the *here and now* (Moreno et al., 1960: 15–16). Encounter is the real basis of the psychotherapeutic process, although transference and counter-transference may be imposed upon it.

There is a sociometric basis for group psychotherapy. When individuals are brought together for group therapy one can only observe them in the initial stages of group formation. The therapist notes the natural groupings by observation. The individuals are locked together by *co-unconscious* material from their common experiences as members of the group (Moreno et al., 1960: 113). "Role reversal puts the cap on the encounter between 'you and I.' It is the final touch of giving unity, identity, and universality to the group" (Moreno et al., 1960: 117).

Spontaneity, creativity and cultural conserve

Spontaneity is a variable degree of adequate response to a situation. To be adequate is to be appropriate, with competency and skill. Spontaneity is related to the readiness to act. The warming up process is the "operational manifestation of spontaneity." Spontaneity is a positive category as opposed to a negative category such as anxiety, fear, and defense.

Creativity is related to the act. The finished product becomes a *cultural conserve* (Moreno et al., 1960: 12). One of Moreno's examples of a cultural conserve is Beethoven's Ninth Symphony. This is a contribution to the culture at large. However, it would appear that Moreno would also consider each creative act of an individual, whether an adequate response to a new situation or a new response to an old situation, as a "cultural conserve" for that individual. It becomes part of the individual's "heritage" in that it serves as a model for future creations of the same type. The creation may be a new word, a new phrase, or a new action.

Catharsis is the realization of potentialities for change and growth, and with this the realization that the significance of the situation has altered.

Role and the cultural atom

Role is a fusion of private and collective elements. It is a unit of "conserved" behavior (one form of cultural conserve). Moreno uses the term "role" in the same way that it is used in social psychology in general, as a set of rights and duties, prescribed by custom or law, associated with a position in society. However, there are two influences on the enactment of a role. One is the way that the role is generally played and the other the variation, the spontaneity that the individual brings to it. An individual is involved in *role taking* when the role is fully established and does not permit individual variation. *Role playing* permits some individual variation. *Role creating* permits a high degree of freedom as a "spontaneity player."

The *self* emerges from roles. There are *psychosomatic roles*, such as the sleeper and eater; *psychodramatic roles*, which are personal versions of social roles, such as a specific mother or teacher; and *social roles*, such as the mother, the teacher. The individual first perceives the role, then enacts it. One can measure the norms for role performance and the degree to which spontaneity is expected in different situations. One can also see how an individual or a group develops roles in psychodrama.

As a test of how well children were learning the expectations for some of the roles that they might be called upon to play in their community, Moreno asked them to enact a role such as mother or father, teacher or doctor. Five members of the community were asked to judge how well the role was enacted. If a child was not able to enact a role, an adult would enact the role in a standardized form to determine if the child could recognize the role. Moreno found that the perception of a role does not automatically mean the ability to enact it. In contrast, a child with a high spontaneity factor is able to elaborate the role (1972: 162–9).

Mead had discussed role taking (Mead, 1950); Moreno adds role playing. There is a resistance to role conserves. An actor wants to adapt the role to the situation. Since society is changing and with it roles, individuals must be able to adapt to change. Moreno developed techniques of role playing to learn how to vitalize and change roles. Moreno asserts that Mead, Freud, and Bergson did not go far enough. They needed someone who was both actor and observer, such as Moreno (Moreno et al., 1960: 80–6).

Each individual is the focus of numerous roles which are related to the roles of other individuals. Just as at all times the individual has a set of friends and enemies, so there is also a set of roles and counter-roles. Each set undergoes continuous change and development. The tangible aspects of the "ego" are the roles in which the individual operates. Moreno designated the set of role relationships of an individual at any given time as the *cultural atom* (1953: 70).

The *cultural atom* is the smallest unit within a cultural pattern. However, cultural atoms are larger than social atoms. Social atoms are nested within cultural atoms. "The socio-atomic organization of a group cannot be separated from its cultural-atomic organization"(Moreno et al., 1960: 53–4).

Dynamics of behavior in groups

Since Moreno drew on his experiences of life directly and indirectly from life as represented in theater, in constructing his approach and techniques for psychodrama, his ideas (summarized in Chapter 3) are in effect a theory of the dynamics of behavior in groups. They can be turned back for analysis of life itself as a series of social dramas. Although Moreno did not consciously do this, others did. Anthropologists described important ceremonies as "social dramas" that give meaning to events, especially those involving transitions of status, while social psychologists indicated that scripts were used as a basis of interaction and the characteristics of action that was "on stage" or "back stage" (Hare, 1985; Hare and Blumberg, 1988).

Moreno's ideas can be used directly for the analysis of the dramaturgical roles that form a basis for social interaction, for example, by identifying the persons playing the roles of director, protagonist, auxiliaries, and audience in everyday events; or by noting the development of the action from the selection of an actable idea, through selecting a stage and scene setting, through developing roles, through enactment, to a final sharing of the new meanings experienced through the action; or by identifying examples of techniques such as role reversal, soliloquy, and doubling (Hare, 1985).[8]

Personality and child development

For Moreno, as noted above in the discussion of the network of interpersonal relations, personality is a reflection of the roles that a person has learned over the course of time. The key factor in personality is the extent to which the individual is spontaneous and can be creative, especially in interpersonal encounters. Thus, to discover the origins of personality in the individual, one must look at the earliest periods of child development. A journal article with Florence Moreno set out a "spontaneity theory of child development" (1944).[9]

From Moreno's perspective, spontaneity and creativity are to be regarded as primary and positive phenomena and not as derivatives of libido or any animal drive. The basic problem for analysis is how the infant "warms up" to the environment and maintains itself from the moment of birth onwards, where the most important parts of the environment are the other individuals with whom the infant interacts. The infant has been prepared for nine months for the act of birth when it must begin to cope successfully with the challenges of the human world.

The first years of life, the "first universe," is a period of "all-identity" where the actions of mother and others are seen as an extension of the infant's own identity. In this period, the infant has a hunger for activity which is so great and consumes so much energy that little energy is left for remembering what is happening, thus "infant amnesia" can be explained. Any memories are flooded out by an overwhelming absorption in the act of the moment. In this period of "all-identity" all things presented to the senses are perceived as one undivided manifold.

During the second period of "all-reality," "the second universe," persons and things are differentiated from each other and from the infant itself. At the beginning of the second universe, at about three years of age, the toddler is able to differentiate fantasy from reality. Social roles provide a connection to the real world and psycho-somatic roles (roles that center on bodily functions such as that of the "eater" or "eliminator") and a connection to the fantasy world. The toddler struggles continually to maintain a balance between behavior patterns related to the real world and those related to the fantasy world.

Spontaneity is the factor that makes it possible for the individual to meet challenging situations adequately when neither memory nor logic is of much value. Human behavior is not entirely predictable because of the spontaneity factor.

When faced with a new situation, the infant, as well as the adult, must "warm up." Often some physical starting mechanisms are the somatic indication of the process of warm up. These indications tend to be centered on areas of the body, around the eyes, nose, mouth, and other body parts. The evidence of warm up indicates that the spontaneity factor has been activated.

Infantile role taking is composed of role giving and role receiving. This is probably experienced by the infant as a gradation from an all-identity phase to a reasonably complete centering of attention on the other person who is playing the complementary role. The emotional learning in infancy is based on this role-reversal process. In the final stage of learning, the child is able to enact the complementary role toward someone else, who in turn is enacting the child's original role. Through the combination of role reversal and attraction or repulsion toward other persons, the infant experiences *tele*, as awareness, feeling for, and understanding.

This chapter has described briefly the major concepts that Moreno (1967) and others (Bischof, 1970) typically included in descriptions of Moreno's theory that focussed on the interpersonal networks in society and how these could be used to enhance individual spontaneity and creativity. As we have noted in the introduction to this chapter, some of these same concepts, such as *tele*, transference, and surplus reality, appear again in Chapter 3 as Moreno applies them in the practice of psychodrama as "social atom repair work" to help people find an optimal placement in a social network for their mental health and that of the community. In addition Moreno describes his method of psychodrama which is, in effect, a theory of group therapy. Some of the key issues in therapy are discussed in Chapter 4 in the summary of Moreno's "lectures". Moreno did not apply his methods directly to counseling, although some years later others suggested how this might be done. For example, Shoobs (1956) and Stein and Callahan (1982) show how psychodramatic techniques may be incorporated in individual counseling, Rockwell (1987) uses sociometry in career counseling, and Kane (1992) considers the potential abuses, limitations, and negative effects of using classical psychodramatic techniques in group counseling. Kane's article is summarized in Chapter 4.

Notes

1 Jiri Nehnevajsa, in an article entitled "Sociometry: decades of growth" (1956) cites many reviews of sociometry. He also cites Jennings and others who have done

research on or extended Moreno's major concepts. He reviews applied research on psychodrama, accounts of clinical applications, and discussions of methods including the sociometric test, sociogram, sociometric indices.

2 We are not including all observations about age, sex, or ethnic group of children since they were based only on US data gathered during the 1940s through 1960s.

3 However, there are some problems with the concept that remain to be sorted out. For example, the number of people involved in a social atom depends on the criterion of choice; more people are chosen on a work criterion than a social criterion. The atom based on a social criterion may be nested within the atom based on a work criterion. There is also the possibility that the social atom of a small child may be included in the social atom of a parent, and thus not form a completely separate unit. A society is not simply the sum of individual social atoms. Although Moreno does distinguish the social atom based on choice from the cultural atom based on role relationships, he does not discuss the intersection of the two sets.

4 There is a problem with ranking. If choices were given as ratings, for example on a five-point scale of attraction, choices one through three might well have the same rated value, yet are listed in some order when the subject is forced to place them in rank order. Moreno was aware of this. In another article on the "organization of the social atom" (Moreno et al., 1960: 56), he notes that a subject may like some number of others equally well. He instructed the subjects (at the Hudson School): "As you choose, weigh carefully whether you would like two or three individuals to live with equally well. You may like two of three persons as 'first choice' . . . ." (Unfortunately, Moreno does not make the connection between this procedure and his analysis of different levels of *tele*.) The fact that two persons place each other first also assumes that they have equal ability to experience *tele*. Moreno's work with the Spontaneity Test indicates that individuals vary in this respect. Thus, one of the persons in the dyad may be experiencing *tele* at that person's maximum, while the other person can experience more *tele* with someone who was not available for choice when the Sociometric Test was given.

5 Helen H. Jennings's "sociometric choice process in personality and group formation" (1960, written 1953) provides a good review of research comparing variables, i.e. choice with rejection, social versus work criteria, sociodramatic performance and sociometric position.

6 Moreno had published an overview of his main concepts with references to the literature as "The sociometric school and the science of man" (1955d), later reprinted in 1956 as an introduction to *Sociometry and the Science of Man*, which represented the contents of volume 18, number 4, of *Sociometry*, the last issue under Moreno's editorship before the journal was transferred to the American Sociological Society.

After completing research at the Hudson School (data published in *Who Shall Survive?*, 1934, and again 1953), Moreno was not involved directly in any sociometric research, although he continued to publish some articles based on the early experience: with Jennings (1938), Jennings and Sargent (1940), Jennings and Stockton (1943), and with Borgatta, new research on sociodrama and sociometry in industry (1951). In 1952 Swanson, Newcomb and Hartley reprinted a selection from *Who Shall Survive?* (1934) on "changes in sex groupings of school children" in *Readings in Social Psychology*. Twenty-year-old data were still news. In 1972 Sahakian reprinted a selection on sociometry from *Who Shall Survive?* (1953) in *Social Psychology: Experimentation, Theory, Research*.

However, Moreno kept abreast of current sociometric research. See "Progress and pitfalls in sociometric theory" (1947a); "Current trends in sociometry" (1952), citations with the 107 hypotheses at the end of *Who Shall Survive?* (1953), and "Old and new trends in sociometry: turning points in small group research" (1954). Moreno predicted new advances in "The birth of a new era for sociometry" (1955c: 268). He was senior editor of a collection of articles on sociometry, *The Sociometry Reader* (Moreno et al., 1960). He continued to emphasize the importance of sociometry as part of the triadic system: "The triadic system, psychodrama–sociometry–group psychotherapy" (1970).

The *Sociometry Reader* (1960), edited by Moreno et al., contains reprints of 64 articles. Twelve of the articles are by Moreno and one is by Moreno and Helen Jennings. All of Moreno's work appears in Part I as "Foundations." Of the additional 51 selections, one-third was first published between 1940 and 1949 and two-thirds were published between 1950 and 1957. During the early 1950s, research on interpersonal choice that related directly to Moreno's ideas had reached its peak. Thus Moreno was familiar with important additions to the sociometric literature up to 1957. However, he did not use the occasion of editing *The Sociometry Reader* to provide an integration of his own research and insights concerning interpersonal choice with the more recent developments. Rather, he chose to reprint a selection of his own articles, providing definitions of concepts, originally published from 1938 through 1955. The reader is left with the task of integrating the various concepts into one theory. The selections provide a shortlist of the concepts that Moreno considered most central to his theory of interpersonal relations. The present summary of Moreno's work makes no attempt to integrate his concepts with the research related to sociometric ideas by his contemporaries, nor did Moreno later summarize work of those who continued to do research through the 1960s and 1970s while the term "sociometry" was still in vogue. However, some indication of the results of research during this period can be gained from the chapter on "interpersonal choice" by Hare (1976) that cites ten reviews of sociometric research and over 400 articles published between 1960 and 1974 relating to interpersonal attraction and choice.

7 Moreno quibbles with Jennings that "leisure time" is not a good criterion because leisure, like friendship, can include so many things. He says that Roethlisberger and Dickson, in their study of *Management and the Worker* (1939), did not ask men or girls who they liked to work with. Whyte, in his observations of *Street Corner Society* (1943), did not warm up subjects to action (Moreno et al., 1960: 121).

8 When Moreno gave a lecture on "Transference, counter-transference and *tele*" as one of a series of lectures during a European tour in the summer of 1954, he asserted that the development of a group therapeutic method depended upon research on concrete groups and their dynamics. "But no group research in the specific sense of the word existed before 1923, the year when the Viennese Stegreif laboratory was founded" (Moreno and Moreno, 1959: 4). However, by the time his lecture was published in 1959 he had added a footnote to suggest that because of the rapid growth of research on small groups, "it may be useful to define 'group therapy research' as dealing directly with therapeutic problems and 'group research' as dealing only indirectly with therapy."

By 1954, Moreno was aware of early experimental research in small groups since he had written an article on "Old and new trends in sociometry: turning points in small group research" published in *Sociometry* (1954) that accompanied the "Bibliography of small group research (from 1900 through 1953)" (Strodtbeck and Hare, 1954) in the same issue. In his article, Moreno shows that he is familiar with the main trends of early group research and considered Gardner Murphy's summary of experimental social psychology (Murphy and Murphy, 1931) as a major force in promoting small group research. However, Moreno still maintains, as he did in his criticism of Bales's (1950) method of using 12 process categories for observation of laboratory groups (Moreno, 1953: 686–8) that any research that does not take into account the perspectives of the actors, as they produce enactments *"in statu nascendi,"* as in the spontaneity theater in Vienna, does not deal with the essence of group interaction. Siding with Moreno, one can note that 40 years later, in the 1990s, most of the laboratory studies of small groups only dealt with the fourth "problem-solving" phase in the development of a group. The first three phases of defining the meaning of the interaction, developing resources, and assigning group roles, if any, were typically all done by the experimenter before the observation began (Hare, 1994: 440–3). Further, in laboratory studies with university students, the student actors are not subject to the restraints of formal organizational roles. Moreno recognized that role was an important determinant in interpersonal behavior in addition to the interpersonal feelings that he designated as *tele*. Thus, although Moreno rarely carried out "experiments" that would come close to satisfying the requirements of research of any of his academic colleagues, it would be fair to say that he was on the right track, although the horse he chose to ride was therapeutic rather than research motivated.

9 The article was reprinted in *Psychodrama: First Volume* (1972). A slightly revised version was reproduced by Wellman (1963) under the title "Basic principles of Moreno's contribution to psychology." One of the advantages of Wellman's version is his summary which we draw on for an outline of the major points in Moreno's theory.

3

Major Contributions to Practice

Moreno's major contribution to the practice of group therapy was to create a new form, *psychodrama*, to deal with individual problems, and a modification, *sociodrama*, to deal with societal problems. Psychodrama has been described as "social atom repair work." In Moreno's view, to be spontaneous and creative, an individual needs to have group support in the form of a "social atom," a network of individuals who are significant others. If someone drops out of the social atom, through death or some other form of separation, the social atom would need to be repaired. New relationships would need to be formed. Sometimes it might be necessary to re-enact traumatic experiences resulting in emotional catharsis and some new insight before this could occur, providing a *catharsis of integration* (Moreno, 1956: 22).

The first part of this chapter will introduce psychodrama, its basic concepts, techniques, adjunctive methods, and Moreno's description of the functions of the director and auxiliary egos as social investigators. Excerpts from three psychodramas and two sociodramas that Moreno conducted are given as examples of his method. The techniques used in psychodrama and sociodrama are essentially the same, only the focus differs. Reference will also be made to the use of psychodrama by others, in its entirety or through the application of some of its techniques, in a variety of settings: schools, industry, and with special clinical populations.

The second part of the chapter deals with sociometry, the method Moreno developed for identifying social atoms and the networks of interpersonal choice that provide psychological undercurrents in groups, organizations, and communities. Since the sociometric method was developed primarily during the research at the Hudson School for Girls, with the collaboration of Helen Jennings, the work at the school will be presented in some detail.

Psychodrama

Moreno's description of psychodrama includes the five main "instruments" of psychodrama (stage, protagonist, director, auxiliary egos, and audience) and their inter-relationships as a drama proceeds through the phases from "warm up" to "sharing." Also included are brief references to some of Moreno's basic concepts (*tele*, surplus reality, catharsis of integration), as well as a list of some of the basic techniques. Senior practitioners of psychodrama in the 1990s, many of whom have been trained directly by Moreno or Zerka Moreno, continue to use this "classic" form, although some have added concepts from other theories as a way of interpreting the information revealed in the psychodrama.

We reproduce here Moreno's own description of psychodrama so that the reader can sense the enthusiasm with which Moreno described the method (Moreno, 1953: 81–7). Note that, following the usage of the time, Moreno refers to the general person as "he." We have inserted the subheadings.

Drama is a transliteration of the Greek [word] which means action, or a thing done. Psychodrama can be defined, therefore, as the science which explores the "truth" by dramatic methods. It deals with interpersonal relations and private worlds. The psychodramatic method uses five instruments: the stage, the subject or actor, the director, the staff of therapeutic aides or auxiliary egos, and the audience.

Stage
The first instrument is the stage. Why a stage? It provides the actor with a living space which is multi-dimensional and flexible to the maximum. The living space of reality is often narrow and restraining, he may easily lose his equilibrium. On the stage he may find it again due to its methodology of freedom – freedom from unbearable stress and freedom for experience and expression. The stage space is an extension of life beyond the reality test of life itself. Reality and fantasy are not in conflict, but both are functions within a wider sphere – the psychodramatic world of objects, persons and events. In its logic the ghost of Hamlet's father is just as real and permitted to exist as Hamlet himself. Delusions and hallucinations are given flesh – embodiment on the stage – and an equality of status with normal sensory perceptions. The architectural design of the stage is made in accord with operational requirements. Its circular forms and levels of the stage, levels of aspiration, pointing out the vertical dimension, stimulate relief from tensions and permit mobility and flexibility of action. The locus of a psychodrama, if necessary, may be designated anywhere, wherever the subjects are, the field of battle, the classroom or the private home. The ultimate resolution of deep mental conflicts requires an objective setting, the psychodrama theater.

Protagonist
The second instrument is the subject or actor [now designated the protagonist]. He is asked to be himself on the stage, to portray his own private world. He is told to be himself, not an actor, as the actor is compelled to sacrifice his own private self to the role imposed upon him by the playwright. Once he is warmed up to the task it is comparatively

easy for the subject to give an account of his daily life in action, as no one has as much authority on himself as himself. He has to act freely, as things rise up in his mind; that is why he has to be given freedom of expression, spontaneity. Next in importance to spontaneity comes the process of the enactment. The verbal level is transcended and included in the level of action. There are several forms of enactment, pretending to be in a role, re-enactment or acting out a past scene, living out a problem presently pressing, creating life on the stage or testing oneself for the future. Further comes the principle of involvement. We have been brought up with the idea that, in test as well as in treatment situations, a minimum of involvement with other persons and objects is the most desirable thing for the subject. In the psychodramatic situation all degrees of involvement take place, from a minimum to a maximum.

In addition comes the principle of realization. The subject is enabled not only to meet parts of himself, but the other persons who take part in his mental conflicts. These persons may be real or illusions. The reality test which is a mere word in other methods is thus actually made true on the stage. The warming up process of the subject to psychodramatic portrayal is stimulated by numerous techniques, only a few of which are mentioned here: self presentation, soliloquy, projection, interpolation of resistance, reversal of roles, double ego, mirror techniques, auxiliary world, realization and psycho-chemical techniques. The aim of these sundry techniques is not to turn the subjects into actors, but rather to stir them up to be on the stage what they *are*, more deeply and explicitly than they appear to be in life reality. The patient has as dramatis personae either the real people of his private world, his wife, his father, his child, etc., or actors portraying them, auxiliary egos.

Director

The third instrument is the director. He has three functions: producer, counsellor and analyst. As a producer he has to be on the alert to turn every clue which the subject offers into dramatic action, to make the line of production one with the life line of the subject, and never to let the production lose rapport with the audience. As director attacking and shocking the subject is at times just as permissible as laughing and joking with him; at times he may become indirect and passive and for all practical purposes the session seems to be run by the subject. As analyst he may complement his own interpretations by responses coming from informants in the audience, husband, parents, children, friends or neighbors.

Auxiliary egos

The fourth instrument is a staff of auxiliary egos. These auxiliary egos or participant actors have a double significance. They are extensions of the director, exploratory and guiding, but they are also extensions of the subject, portraying the actual or imagined personae of their life drama. The functions of the auxiliary ego are threefold: the function of the actor, portraying roles required by the subject's world; the function of the counsellor, guiding the subject; and the function of the social investigator.

Audience

The fifth instrument is the audience. The audience itself has a double purpose. It may serve to help the subject or, being itself helped by the subject on the stage, the audience becomes the problem. In helping the subject it is a sounding board of public opinion. Its responses and comments are as extemporaneous as those of the subject, they may vary from laughter to violent protest. The more isolated the subject is, for instance, because his drama on the stage is shaped by delusions and hallucinations, the more important becomes, to him, the presence of an audience which is willing to accept and understand him. When the audience is helped by the subject, thus becoming the subject itself, the situation is reversed. The audience sees itself, that is, one of its collective syndromes portrayed on the stage.

Phases in psychodrama

In any discussion of psychodrama the important dynamics which operate should be considered. In the first phase of psychodramatic process the director may meet with some resistance from the subject. In most cases the resistance against being psychodramatized is small or nil. Once a subject understands the degree to which the production is of his own making he will cooperate. The fight between the director and the subject is in the psychodramatic situation extremely real; to an extent that they have to assess each other like two battlers, facing each other in a situation of great stress and challenge. Each of them have to draw spontaneity and cunning from their resources. Positive factors which shape the relationship and interaction in the reality of life itself exist; spontaneity, productivity, the warming up process, *tele* and role processes.

The psychodramatist, after having made so much ado to get the subject started, recedes from the scene; frequently he does not take any part in it, at times he is not even present. From the subject's point of view his object of transference, the director, is pushed out of the situation. The retreat of the director gives the subject the feeling that he is the winner. Actually it is nothing but the preliminary warm up before the big bout. To the satisfaction of the subject other persons enter into the situation, persons who are nearer to him, like his delusions and hallucinations. He knows them so much better than this stranger, the director. The more they are in the picture the more he forgets him and the director wants to be forgotten, at least for the time being. The dynamics of this forgetting can be easily explained. Not only does the director leave the scene of operation, the auxiliary egos step in and it is between them that his share of *tele*, transference and empathy is divided. In the course of the production it becomes clear that *transference is nothing by itself, but the pathological portion of a universal factor, tele,* operating in the shaping and balancing of all interpersonal relations.

As the subject takes part in the production and warms up to the figures and figure-heads of his own private world he attains tremendous satisfactions which take him far beyond anything he has ever experienced; he has invested so much of his own limited energy in the images of his perceptions of father, mother, wife, children, as well as in certain images which live a foreign existence within him, delusions and hallucinations of all sorts, that he has lost a great deal of spontaneity, productivity and power for himself. They have taken his riches away and he has become poor, weak and sick. The psychodrama gives back to him all the investments he had made in the extraneous adventures of his mind. He takes his father, mother, sweethearts, delusions and hallucinations unto himself and the energies which he has invested in them, they return by actually living through the role of his father or his employer, his friends or his enemies; by reversing the roles with them he is already learning many things about them which life does not provide him. When he can be the persons he hallucinates, not only do they lose their power and magic spell over him but he gains their power for himself. His own self has an opportunity to find and reorganize itself, to put the elements together which may have been kept apart by insidious forces, to integrate them and to attain a sense of power and of relief, a "catharsis of integration" (in difference from a catharsis of abreaction). It can well be said that the psychodrama provides the subject with a new and more extensive experience of reality, a *"surplus" reality*, a gain which at least in part justifies the sacrifice he made by working through a psychodrama production.

The next phase in a psychodrama comes into play when the audience drama takes the place of the production. The director vanished from the scene at the end of the first phase; now the production itself vanishes and with it the auxiliary egos; the good helpers and genii who have aided him so much in gaining a new sense of power and clarity. The subject is now divided in his reactions; on the one hand he is sorry that it is all gone, on the other he feels cheated and mad for having made a sacrifice whose justification he does not see completely. The subject becomes dynamically aware of the presence of the audience. In the beginning of the session he was angrily or happily aware of it. In the warming up of the production he became oblivious to its existence but now he sees it again, one by one, strangers and friends. His feelings of shame and guilt reach their climax. However, as he was warming up to the production the audience before him was warming up too. But when he came to the end they were just beginning. The *tele*-empathy-transference complex undergoes a third realignment of forces; it moves from the stage to the audience, initiating among the audio-egos intensive relations. As the strangers from the group begin to rise and relate their feelings as to what they have learned from the production, he gains a new sense of catharsis, a group catharsis; *he has given love and now they are giving back love to him.* [This phase is now called "sharing."] Whatever his psyche is now, it was molded originally by the group; by means of psychodrama it returns to the group and now the members of the audience are sharing their experiences with him as he has shared his with them.

The description would not be complete if we would not discuss briefly the role the director and the egos play in the warm up of the session. The theoretical principle of psychodrama is that the director acts directly upon the level of the subject's spontaneity – obviously it makes little difference to the operation whether one calls the subject's spontaneity his "unconscious" – that the subject enters actually the areas of objects and persons, however confused and fragmented, to which his spontaneous energy is related. He is not satisfied, like the analyst, to observe the subject and translate symbolic behavior into understandable, scientific language; he enters as a participant-actor, armed with as many hypothetic insights as possible, into the spontaneous activities of the subject, to talk to him in the spontaneous languages of signs and gestures, words and actions which the subject has developed. Psychodrama does not require a theatrical setting, a frequent misunderstanding; it is done *in situ* – that is, wherever the subject is found.

According to psychodramatic theory a considerable part of the psyche is not language-ridden, it is not infiltrated by the ordinary, significant language symbols. Therefore, bodily contact with subjects, if it can be established, touch, caress, embrace, handshake, sharing in silent activities, eating, walking or other activities, are an important preliminary to psychodramatic work itself. Bodily contact, body therapy and body training continue to operate in the psychodramatic situation. An elaborate system of production techniques has been developed by means of which the director and his auxiliary egos push themselves into the subject's world, populating it with figures extremely familiar to him, with the advantage, however, that they are not delusionary but half imaginary, half real. Like good and bad genii they shock and upset him at times, at other times they surprise and confront him. He finds himself, as if trapped, in a near-real world. *He sees himself acting, he hears himself speaking, but his actions and thoughts, his feelings and perceptions do not come from him, they come, strangely enough, from another person, the psychodramatist, and from other persons, the auxiliary egos, the doubles and mirrors of his mind.*

Excerpts from three psychodramas

An adolescent

This psychodrama was directed by Moreno in 1939 on the stage of his theater at Beacon, New York. The participants in the drama were Bill (the adolescent), his parents, a social worker, and auxiliary egos drawn from the audience (Moreno and Moreno, 1969: 39, 46–9, 52–8). Before the drama begins, the social worker moves to the stage and gives the audience some of the background to Bill's problem. Bill is 14½ years old. He has been in reform school for four weeks. His father is an independent physician and fairly well-to-do. Bill has been disturbed since the birth of his younger brother two years before. Since then he has been a truant from schools and special camps. At the reform school he was said to masturbate excessively and expose himself to the housemother and the other boys.

Next, Moreno interviews Bill while they sit together on the middle level of the psychodrama stage. Moreno asks Bill why he ran away from school. Bill is then asked to act out a scene that took place after he had run away from Military School when a judge sends him to reform school. In the first scene Bill plays himself and an auxiliary plays the judge. Before the scene begins, Moreno asks them to go backstage for preparation; they then come back on stage where they arrange tables and chairs to simulate the judge's chambers.

In contemporary psychodrama, the actors remain on stage. "Scene setting" is done by the protagonist in response to questions from the director, sometimes "reversing roles" with objects in the setting, to warm up the protagonist and give the director and audience a feeling for the mood of the situation or to supply background information. Auxiliaries are introduced to the main themes in their roles through "role reversal" with the protagonist.

In Bill's case, the auxiliary makes several attempts to simulate the behavior of the judge, with corrections from Bill, before they are able to begin the short scene, although Bill continues to make "out of role" comments:

> *Judge*: No, I can't send you back to Military School. I'm going to send you to Montrose for a rest. We'll see if you can make good there before we can let you return to Military School. What do you say to that?
> *Bill*: Yes, your Honor. I'm sorry for what I did.
> *Judge*: Have you anything else to say?
> *Bill*: No.
> *Judge*: Why did you run away? Why did you do all those things?
> *Bill*: [*out of role*] He didn't say that. I said to the judge [*back in the role*]: Let me go home, your Honor, I want to go to school there.
> *Judge*: You want to live at home and go to school there?
> *Bill*: Yes. I don't like Military School.
> *Judge*: Then why did you go to Military School in the first place?
> *Bill*: I wanted to see what it was like.
> *Judge*: [*looking over some papers on his desk*] I see that your record in public, private and Military School shows that you play truant; and in Military School you steal military uniforms. Is that right?
> *Bill*: [*out of role, dejectedly*] Yes. That's why they sent me to Montrose.
> *Judge*: Now, I want you to promise that you won't run away from Montrose, and make good there.
> *Bill*: Yes, your Honor.
> *Judge*: That's fine. [*End of scene.*]

Moreno then asks Bill to "role reverse" with the judge, taking the judge's chair and, by playing both judge and himself, re-enacting the scene. Moreno continues his interview with Bill concerning his feelings about the judge, his relationship with his girlfriend, and difficulties at Military School. Moreno asks the social worker about his meeting with Bill's mother. Bill says that he saw the social worker when he arrived at their home. Moreno tells Bill and the social worker that he would like to see what happened. Bill, the social worker, and an auxiliary who will play Bill's mother are sent backstage to prepare. They enact two short scenes. In the first Bill plays his father. The scene is the downstairs office of the father. Bill, in the role of father, is speaking angrily to the auxiliary in the role of his wife.

> *Father*: Stella, for the Lord's sake, stop crying. It drives me crazy. I can't work here.
> *Mother*: I'm so desperate about Bill. [*Weeps*] You just don't care, you have no heart. My mother says . . . [*Weeps again*].
> *Father*: Your mother . . . why do you always have to bring her into everything? [*Slams door.*] [*End of scene.*]

Bill explains that the next scene involves the meeting between the social worker and Bill's mother with Bill in the background. This scene is played out with eight exchanges between the social worker and Bill's mother (an auxiliary) with one interjection by Bill.

Moreno continues the interview with Bill, asking about money he took from his father's pocket. Bill admits that he took a few pieces of silver but insists he intended to return it. Bill says that he works and has had a bank account since childhood. He tells Moreno about his love for fantastic stories, ancient history, and miracles. Last night he dreamed of a miracle. Moreno suggests that they act it out.

Bill warms up for the next scene by walking around the stage describing the room where he sleeps. He says that he suddenly wakes up from the dream and looks around. At this point, Moreno assigns an auxiliary to play the part of a double for Bill, as Bill II.

> *Moreno*: Here is your double, another Bill, yourself, acting exactly the same way you do. He is in bed next to you, and suddenly awakes from a dream.
> *Bill I* [*Bill himself*]: Who are you?
> *Bill II* [*the auxiliary*]: I am Bill, too.
> *Bill I*: I had a strange dream.
> *Bill II*: So did I, very strange.
> *Bill I*: It was like this. [*Starts to get up.*]
> *Bill II*: I was out of bed. [*Gets up too, both do the same thing. Bill II copies the motions of Bill I.*]
> *Bill I*: I notice that you are naked.
> *Bill II*: You're naked too, didn't you know?
> *Bill I*: I like to sleep in the nude.
> *Bill II*: My father does too.
> *Bill I*: I don't like to wear pajamas, but I wear my underwear. I may have walked around in my underwear.

The action continues with Bill talking to his double about sleeping nude, masturbating, being caught nude in bed by the housemother, taking fruit, taking money, his feeling that his mother wanted a girl, the death of his grandfather whom he loved, and his fear that he might be changed into a girl. At the end of the scene Bill says to Moreno: "There are all kinds of things I think about, life and other things."

Moreno reverts to the interview format, asking mainly about his concern that he might be changed into a girl and his interest in becoming a scientist or doctor. Moreno suggests: "If you are a scientist–doctor nobody can change you into a girl, eh?" *Bill*: "Yeah. That's why I want to be a doctor myself." Moreno signals the end of the session with: "Well, Bill, I thank you. It was a fine session. But our time is up, we have to close."

In an analysis that follows in the text, Moreno notes that this was the first of a series of 12 sessions at weekly intervals. At the end of the treatment, Bill entered a military school, was later admitted to college, served in the United States Army honorably, and at the time of writing was on the way to becoming a doctor of medicine.

Moreno stresses that the first session is the most difficult to handle because of its strategic importance. If the director makes a small tactical error the whole treatment program may be blocked. In this session, the opening interview was extremely long because of suspicion and distrust on the part of the subject of therapists in general.

The director has two aims: first, to place the client at ease; and, secondly, to discover a problem and a situation where the action may begin. This is the search for an "actable idea." Although, in this case, the first two scenes with the judge and the social worker seem to follow naturally from the opening interview, Moreno notes that the third scene came from a surprise clue that Bill had a dream the previous night. It is for these deeper clues that the director has to wait patiently. However, the director has to be ready for such clues by learning as much as possible about the case beforehand. Diagnosis and treatment may go hand in hand; a diagnostic clue may be discerned on the spot and immediately used for therapeutic aims.

Psychodrama of a marriage

This session was also held in the psychodrama theater at Beacon, New York in 1939 (Moreno and Moreno, 1969: 84–104). Frank and Ann, a couple from a nearby university, have come to visit the theater and have expressed an interest in the work. Moreno begins the session by suggesting that the best way to understand the meaning of the theater is to act in it. He asks Frank if he has a problem that he would like to work out on the stage.

> *Frank*: [*Goes up to the stage after some hesitation.*] Yes, I do have a problem in reference to my marriage. We had a happy marriage. My wife and I were working towards a goal. I achieved what I wanted but during my course of study in Boston I met a young woman with whom I fell in love. She is coming to New York next week. I would like to know what to do when she comes.
>
> *Moreno*: Is your wife present?
>
> *Frank*: Yes, there she sits. [*Points to his wife who is asked to come up on the stage. She is startled by this development. The woman who brought the couple to the theater is also surprised by the sudden turn of the situation.*]
>
> *Moreno*: Does you wife know about your relationship with this girl?
>
> *Frank*: She does not know everything. But she has been very understanding. That's why I told her about next week.

Moreno suggests that Frank and Ann play out a scene that would indicate their relationship at present. They decide on a scene at their home a week before. Moreno tells them to talk as usual, but also to use "asides" in the form of soliloquies in which they say what they are thinking. At first, since they have never had any experience with psychodrama, they report what happened. Moreno tells them not to report and not to tell the story, but to re-live it as it actually happened. They begin again.

> *Frank*: Well, what are you thinking about?
>
> *Ann*: Do you know what day this is?
>
> *Frank*: Yes, it's our sixth wedding anniversary. [*A pause as he gathers himself to speak of the real matter at hand.*] This business next week, how do you feel about it?
>
> *Ann*: It's hard to say. I hope you believe now that I understand? [*She chokes.*]
>
> *Frank*: Yes, I do. Do you mind talking about it?
>
> *Ann*: [*Makes an effort to pull herself together.*] Not any more. I feel that I can without misunderstanding.
>
> *Frank*: What do you think went wrong between us?

The session continues for nine pages of printed text. Frank and Ann discuss who was dependent and who was independent. Frank did not want to have a child since it would tie down the future. Ann wanted a child. They discuss Frank's feeling for the other woman, Ellen.

Ann takes a seat in the audience and Moreno asks Frank to pick an auxiliary to play Ellen. Frank and the woman playing Ellen go backstage to warm up for the scene for about two minutes. Moreno directs a scene in which Frank and Ellen are having breakfast in a hotel where they had been spending the past three days. They discuss Ann and her reactions. This scene is recorded as having lasted 17 minutes.

Frank and the auxiliary take their seats and Moreno has a discussion with Ann and Frank about the fact that they have been married for six years and have not had a baby. Moreno asks Frank about his relationship with his three younger sisters and about the early days of his marriage. He also asks Ann about her immediate family. This conversation goes on for another three pages of text. At the end of the session, Moreno observes that from what he saw on the stage he judges Frank to be a man of great determination, who can carry things through up to a point, but cannot finish. Frank seems to want the women to make the decisions for him, either for his wife to say that she would not stand in his way or for Ellen to say that their affair was only temporary and that he could go back to his wife. Moreno concludes the session with: "One often finds men who are able to make a start, and to develop a situation and make a 'mess,' but who are unable to end the situation. The psychodrama can help you people to make a decision."

A second session is held with Frank and Ann and two auxiliaries. Frank and Ann play the scene that occurred in their bedroom a few days before the weekend that Frank was to spend with Ellen. Frank says that he had made a decision and had written to Ellen that the relationship with her would not work out. However, he also says that he wants a divorce from Ann. Ann does not want to give up the relationship. The scene lasts 11 minutes.

For the next scene, the woman auxiliary plays Ellen. They re-enact Frank's meeting with Ellen when she arrives in New York for the weekend. They move through several locations, the train station, the hotel, a restaurant, with a few lines exchanged in each situation. The total scene lasts ten minutes.

Moreno then tells Frank that he would like to see the crucial scene which took place just before Ellen left to go home. Frank complains that it is difficult because the auxiliary is so different from the real Ellen. Moreno asks if he would prefer to act with someone else.

Ann: [*spontaneously*] Can I do it?
Frank: [*vindictively*] My God, No!

Moreno directs Frank and the auxiliary to go backstage to warm up for the scene. The scene, which lasts five minutes, is mainly Frank telling "Ellen" about the psychodrama he had with Moreno. Moreno then conducts a long interview with Frank concerning his relationship with Ellen. Ann adds an occasional comment.

After Frank and Ann leave the theater, Moreno has a few words with the auxiliaries. He warns them that they must guard against personal bias or taking sides. Whomever Frank finally chooses, they may need to help the other woman deal with the separation.

A transcript of a third session is also provided (1969: 104–32). The session is held with Frank and Ellen who enact a number of scenes, beginning with their first meeting. At the conclusion of the session, Moreno observes: "The test of love and marriage is its productivity as a team. The next session will show whether the team of Frank and Ellen is more productive than that of Frank and Ann." Unfortunately for the involved reader, no more sessions are published.

Psychodrama of a dream

In contrast to the work of Freud and others, Moreno notes that this psychodrama provides an example of production techniques for the enactment of dreams, rather than on their analysis and interpretation (1951a, see also Fox, 1987: 185–99).

The patient, Martin, had come to Beacon for treatment, sometimes with his wife, once a week during the summer of 1946. Two days after his second treatment session the dream took place. The psychodrama was recorded using a wire recorder and an observer in the audience who noted the actions and interactions between the dream characters. Present at the session were a staff of trained auxiliary egos and six patients from the sanatorium. After the production, the patients were encouraged to relate themselves to the production and to describe some of their own dreams.

At the start of the session, Moreno and Martin are sitting on the middle, or interview level, of the psychodrama stage. As the action begins, Moreno takes Martin's hand and leads him to the top level of the stage. Here, in answer to questions from Moreno, Martin sets the stage to represent the room in his father-in-law's house where the dream took place. Moreno changes the lighting on the stage to a soft blue. Martin lies down on several chairs that represent a bed. Moreno asks him to try to fall asleep slowly. Moreno closes Martin's eyes with his hands and gently strokes his hair.

Moreno: Do you see the dream?
Martin: Yes.
Moreno: The sequence of the dream? [*Martin nods his head.*]
Moreno: Try to concentrate and try to visualize it as best you can, but don't tell us anything about it. Just concentrate on the dream. Do you have it now? Let it pass just like a sequence of scenes through your mind. Do you have it? [*Moreno's voice is suggestive, gentle and softer than usual.*]

Martin: Yes I have it. [*Is beginning to look more at ease.*]
Moreno: Do you see the people in it? Do you see the media, the environment in which it takes place? [*Continues to stroke Martin's head, his hair, forehead, helping him to relax.*]

Martin begins to recount his dream. He is standing in the dining room. Moreno has him stand. He is near the kitchen door. Moreno tells him to move towards the door. What does he see? There is a group of women. Moreno calls auxiliaries to the stage to play the parts of the women as they are identified. The women include family members, their friends, and his wife.

Moreno: [*Explaining to Martin, the auxiliary egos and all the audience present*] You see, Martin, the characters in your dream are like wax figures on the stage; the auxiliary egos representing them move, act, speak, or spring to life only as and when you, the dreamer, direct them. They have no life of their own, therefore you tell them what to do. What are they discussing?

The women are discussing his wife's visit to a doctor. As Martin identifies particular women who have spoken, Moreno prompts the auxiliary to repeat the line and continue to improvise interaction with Martin when called on. Martin becomes angry with the women.

Martin: Then all of a sudden they reject me. They push me out of the room.
Moreno: Push him out of the room! [*Five women push him out, off the stage. Martin resists.*]

The enactment of the dream continues as Martin goes to a drugstore where he sees doctor's instruments. He telephones his wife who says she is taking a bath before going to see the doctor. Now Martin is in a grocery store. Moreno asks how he feels. Martin says that he feels that he is about to lose something. That he was hoping that he would not have to visit the doctor with his wife. But now he knows that she is taking a bath in preparation. He concludes: "I feel very unhappy. I have the urge to do something. I raise my arm as if to hit someone. At this point the dream ends."

Moreno walks up on the stage to interview Martin. Moreno has Martin go back to bed and wake up from the dream. Martin is directed to re-enact writing down the dream, as he had done, and then return to bed. Martin says that he slept without dreaming. But Moreno, using gently relaxing touches, asks him what he sees. He sees his mother-in-law trying to help him open a box. Then there is a soiled rug that he wants to throw out, but his wife does not want him to. With a mixture of enactments assisted by auxiliaries and interviews, Moreno takes Martin through a series of related dream fragments.

Moreno suggests to Martin that he is annoyed with his wife because she takes a bath and dresses up before going to see the doctor as if she were preparing herself for a sexual encounter. At the end of the session, Martin makes the connection that since Moreno is now his doctor, and he did not bring his wife to the session, that: "Maybe now the situation is reversed. Now it is she who is anxious to come to my doctor. I'm trying to keep her away from you, just as she was trying to keep me away from her gynecologist. It's sweet revenge." Moreno and Martin both smile and shake hands. Moreno ends the session with a discussion of the other patients' responses to the dream.

Sociodrama

Moreno's description of sociodrama will be followed by two examples of sociodramas. The first, dealing with the acceptance of a black family in a white community, represents a social problem that could have occurred anywhere in the United Sates in 1945 when the sociodrama was conducted. In contrast, the re-enactment of the Eichmann trial is reminiscent of the "spontaneity theater" in Vienna and the "living newspaper" in New York in that it dealt with a current event. The session was conducted in 1961. It represents Moreno's ultimate aim of being able to provide, through socio-drama, a catharsis for a whole society and thus prevent it from developing a "sociosis" (the group counterpart of "psychosis"). Just as *psychiatry* helps the individual deal with neurosis, so *sociatry* would help the group deal with sociosis.

Sociatry
Moreno set out the aims of sociatry (1953: 379):

> The imbalances within the social atom and their reflection upon the development of psychological currents and networks give social psychiatry a nosological basis and differentiate it as a discipline from psychiatry proper. *Psychiatric concepts as neurosis and psychosis are not applicable to socioatomic processes. A group of individuals may become "sociotic" and the syndrome producing this condition can be called "sociosis."*
>
> The initiation of the science of sociatry coincides with the critical historical situation of mankind in the middle of our century. The aim of the new science is prophylaxis, diagnosis and treatment of mankind, of group and intergroup relations and particularly to explore how groups can be formed which propel themselves into realization via techniques of freedom *without* the aid of sociatry or psychiatry. The secret aim of

sociatry, and of all science, is to help mankind in the realization of its aims and ultimately to become unnecessary and perish.

Sociodrama defined

Moreno's description of sociodrama is as follows (1953: 87–9):

Sociodrama has been defined as a deep action method dealing with inter-group relations and collective ideologies. The procedure in the development of a sociodrama differs in many ways from the procedure which I have described as psychodramatic. In a psychodramatic session, the attention of the director and his staff are centered upon the individual and his private problems. As these are unfolded before a group, the spectators are affected by the psychodramatic acts in proportion to the affinities existing between their own context of roles, and the role context of the central subject. Even the so-called group approach in psychodrama is in the deeper sense individual-centered. The audience is organized in accord with a mental syndrome which all participating individuals have in common, and the aim of the director is to reach every individual in his own sphere, separated from the other. He is using the group approach only to reach actively more than one individual in the same session. The group approach in psychodrama is concerned with a group of *private* individuals, which makes the group itself, in a sense, private. Careful planning and organizing the audience is here indispensable because there is no outward sign indicating which individual suffers from the same mental syndrome and can share the same treatment situation.

The true subject of sociodrama is the *group*. It is not limited by a special number of individuals, it can be as many persons as there are human beings anywhere, or at least of as many as belong to the same culture. Sociodrama is based upon the tacit assumption that the group formed by the audience is already organized by the social and cultural roles which in some degree all the carriers of the culture share. It is therefore incidental who the individuals are, or of whom the group is composed, or how large their number is. It is the group as a whole which has been put on the stage to work out its problem, because the group in sociodrama corresponds to the individual in psychodrama. Sociodrama, therefore, in order to become effective, has to assay the difficult task of developing deep action methods, in which the working tools are representative types within a given culture and not private individuals. Catharsis in the sociodrama differs from catharsis in the psychodrama. The psychodramatic approach deals with personal problems principally and aims at personal catharsis; the sociodramatic approach deals with social problems and aims at social catharsis.

The concept underlying this approach is the recognition that *man is a roleplayer*, that every individual is characterized by a certain range of roles which dominate his behavior, and that every culture is characterized by a certain set of roles which it imposes with a varying degree of success upon its membership.

The problem is how to bring cultural order to view by dramatic methods. Even if full information could be attained by observation and analysis, it has become certain that observation and analysis are inadequate tools for exploring the more sophisticated aspects of inter-cultural relations, and that deep action methods are indispensable. Moreover, the latter have proven to be of indisputable value and un-replaceable because they can, in the form of sociodrama, *explore as well as treat in one stroke*, the conflicts which have arisen between two separate cultural orders, and at the same time, by the same action, undertaking to change the attitude of members of one culture versus the members of the other. Furthermore, it can reach large groups of people, and by using radio and television it can affect millions of local groups and neighborhoods, in which inter-cultural conflicts and tensions are dormant or in the initial stages of open warfare. Therefore, the potentialities of drama research and role research for giving clues to methods by which public opinion and attitudes can be influenced or changed are still unrecognized and unresolved.

Excerpts from two sociodramas

The black–white problem

This sociodrama was conducted in a large university in the United States in 1945 as part of an intercultural workshop (1972: 367–83).[1] The terms referring to race used by Moreno have been changed to reflect current usage.

As Moreno enters the auditorium, he sees an African-American couple in the audience. He invites them to come up on the stage. Moreno has apparently given the couple some direction, or they have seen a sociodrama before, because in the protocol they im-mediately begin to speak as if in answer to a question.

> *Richard*: I am Richard Cowley, this is my wife Margaret. I'm forty years old, my wife is thirty five.
> *Moreno*: Where do you live Mr Cowley?
> *Richard*: I have lived in a great many places . . . Here is the house [*points to the center of the stage*].
> *Moreno*: Why not introduce us to your home? How do you get in?
> *Richard*: I'm sorry, I can't introduce you.
> *Moreno*: Why?
> *Richard*: I don't bring white people into my home.

Moreno continues the interview, finding out about the house after Margaret agrees to show him around. Moreno asks about the furniture and about their books. Moreno asks Margaret if they have had any troubles lately. Margaret says yes, occasionally. Moreno then suggests a scene in which they have just returned from the university where they are studying. He asks them to talk about the white people at the university.

Richard: It would be pretty hard to talk about the people at the university. I thought you wanted problems.

Richard and Margaret sit down. After some opening conversation about graduate student housing, Richard speaks of a man he met at the university who told about a magazine article concerning African-American soldiers in the Second World War who had not done well in combat. The white explanation was that they were "primitive people." Richard and Margaret recounted the African-American version which was that the soldiers had a morale problem because all their top officers, who were white, were not kindly disposed.

At this point a white woman enters, an auxiliary ego sent up by Moreno.

Mrs White: [*out of breath*] How do you do, I am Mrs White. I wonder if you have seen a little boy running through here. I am terribly distressed. My boy was just hit by a little black boy. Have you seen a little boy?
Margaret: Was it your boy that was running? Who are you looking for?
Mrs White: The black boy came up and hit my boy. We can't find him.
Margaret: Nobody has come here.

Mrs White makes three more statements in which she asserts that the boy who hit her son was a nasty little youngster, that the Cowleys are probably trying to protect their neighbors, and that they do not want to help. She leaves. The Cowleys are discussing what happened and another happening at the university when Mrs White reappears. This time she presents herself as a person from the West who has always been interested in the problems of the African-American. She invites the Cowleys to supper. They try to warn her off, saying that it may be difficult for other guests, but Mrs White insists. The Cowleys finally agree. Moreno intervenes at this point to interview the Cowleys.

Moreno: Have you ever been treated this way, or do you know of any similar incident, Mr Cowley?
Richard: I think I know what you are after. I am not going to answer you from my belief. It was this – that reaction – it was an almost unbelievable thing – such a shocking thing.
Moreno: Do you mean to say you never met a white man who has treated you in an acceptable way?
Richard: [*excited*] Certainly I did, but for a *white woman* to come into my home in the South is shocking; it is sufficient reason for me to behave as I did.

The interview continues. Richard explains that his reaction would be different in the South than in the West. Moreno asks if Richard learned anything from the psychodrama. Richard responds that he had a block about psychodrama, but "I *live* this thing – it isn't acting." However, he notes that in a few days Moreno will be gone and he will still have to live with the situation. Moreno then asks the Cowleys many questions about their style of life, where they work, who they voted for, the books they read, and their house. A note in the protocol tells us that Moreno is looking for a new scene, a scene in the future.

> *Moreno*: Our world is a world of change. You are both young people. Today is 1945. Let's go to 1957. Where do you expect to be in 1957?

In a scene in the study of their new home the Cowleys discuss the events of the year. They are now well off financially, laws have been passed making discrimination in employment illegal, progress has been made. The scene is closed by an observation by Margaret.

> *Margaret*: Let's go to bed. I'm getting sleepy.

Moreno thanks the Cowleys for their cooperation and asks them not to leave the session until the discussion with the audience is finished. Moreno then asks members of the audience to vote on the extent to which they identified with the Cowleys and Mrs White and their attitudes. He notes that there are many audiences in the United States and each might vote differently depending upon their racial, gender, occupational, and religious differences. Moreno asks several members of the audience what brought them to the performance and then calls for a show of hands of others with similar backgrounds or reasons, these he identifies as social networks. Later he says that he could draw a diagram of the social networks in the audience.

Moreno asks if there is anyone who would have enacted the role of Mrs White differently. Three volunteers each give a new version of the role. Would anyone have acted differently from the Cowleys? Two African-American couples come to the stage, but although each intended to act differently, what they produce on the stage is an amazing replica of the Cowley presentation.

In his analysis of the drama, Moreno notes that every person has an *identity* that leads him or her to believe that all people in the same category share a common identity. Thus, people with similar identities form an "in group," the others an "out group." However, it is possible to identify with another's identification, as presumably Mrs White learned to treat blacks as they were seen by her son, who saw them only as playmates. Moreno says that there may be *subjective identification*, the projection of an individual, usually unreal, feeling into another individual. According to Freud, identification is due to the transference of the image of, for instance, one's own father, the image of authority and omnipotence, upon a stranger. In *objective* identification, the experience of an image or situation of another person is fairly accurate. Moreno concludes that to become better acquainted with the African-American family, the audience would need to know them not only intellectually and as neighbors, but also psychodramatically by working together on the psychodrama stage (1972: 367–83).

Psychodrama and sociodrama of Judaism and the Eichmann trial

This combined psychodrama and sociodrama was enacted during the 1961 annual meeting of the American Academy of Psychodrama and Group Psychotherapy, of which Moreno was the director. The meeting was held just prior to the meeting of the American Psychiatric Association. At the time, Eichmann was on trial for his part in the extermination of Jews in death camps during the Second World War. The participants in the drama, as auxiliary egos, were people who had been in training with Moreno, including his wife, Zerka. Moreno does not provide an account of the actual mock trial of Eichmann in detail (1961). Rather, a three-page note is written as a memorandum to the presiding judge at the Eichmann trial and other officials including the Prime Minister of Israel. It is also addressed to the people of Israel, all contemporaries around the globe, and to Adolf Eichmann.

In an introduction, Moreno explains that "this psychodrama is not identical with a court of law, but the re-enactment of Eichmann's life and deeds within the framework of Judaism. It is not a theater, but the representation of the experiences of actual victims." He asserts that it is not only Eichmann who is on trial, but all those who have been affected by the events of the holocaust, including survivors of the camps as well as Germans who were directly or indirectly involved; even those who opposed the Nazi system; indeed, all those "with distantly involved emotions and astonishment."

Moreno recommends that Eichmann be taken out of his cage at the actual trial and be given the full range of the courtroom to act out crucial episodes in his life, under the direction of a psychodramatist with a staff of auxiliary egos who will play the roles of persons who were important to him as well as act out with him his delusions and hallucinations. Eichmann would be asked to reverse roles with all Jews that had been his victims.

The enactment should lead to a process of catharsis, not only for Eichmann, but for all those involved in any way. Moreno recommends the use of television, motion pictures, and simultaneous psychodramatic re-trials in many parts of the world to make a mass co-experience possible. However, the entire drama should not last longer than five hours, enacted in two sessions of two and a half hours each, at the end of the formal court proceedings. "The entire Eichmann trial may find in the psychodrama of Judaism its true climax."

In 1965 Moreno directed a psycho/sociodrama along similar lines, again before an audience at the annual meeting of the Academy of Psychodrama and Group Psychotherapy. Moreno published a notice of the forthcoming event in 1964 (Moreno, 1964a) and an account appeared in *Time* magazine (15 May, 1965, p. 64). This was an enactment of the trial of Jack Ruby who had killed Lee Harvey Oswald who had been accused of assassinating President John F. Kennedy. Before the event Moreno had asked the judge at Ruby's trial to let Ruby play himself on the psychodrama stage. The judge refused. The defense council was also invited to be present to play his own part. Although he accepted, he did not arrive for the event.

In his announcement of the proposed drama, Moreno said that "The psychodramatic trial . . . is a form of scientific mass psychotherapy. It will pave the way for a mass catharsis and a better understanding of the problems of our perennial melting pot now in a turmoil without parallel in its history" (Moreno, 1964a: 62). *Time* magazine recorded "Most orthodox psychiatrists are skeptical of psychodrama, but at the play's end, the entire audience of 400 seemed to feel better – as if the doctors of the mind had needed to get something off their minds."

Rules for the conduct of a psychodrama

In *Psychodrama, Third Volume*, Zerka Moreno records a set of 15 rules for the conduct of a psychodrama (Moreno, Z. T., 1965; reprinted in Moreno and Moreno, 1969: 233–8). For each rule, a one-sentence description of the rule is followed by a short summary of her explanation of the rule. As an introduction, Zerka notes that the then growing demand for skilled workers in psychodrama had made it necessary to list the fundamental rules. The rules are written as they would apply to a psychodrama focused on the treatment of one individual, where there is a patient and director, and sometimes auxiliary egos. But the rules also apply when psychodrama is used as a method of group treatment, where other patients in the group may serve as auxiliary egos for one another, who in turn derive therapeutic benefit from the auxiliary ego function, intensifying the learning for all those present.

(1) *Action* "The subject (patient, client, protagonist) acts out his conflicts, instead of talking about them." To this end a psychodrama stage may be used, which can induce more intense involvement, although any informal space can be used. The process requires as a minimum a director and at least one trained auxiliary ego for maximum learning, although the director may act as an auxiliary if no other person is available.

(2) *Here and now* "The subject or patient acts 'in the here and now,' regardless of when the actual incident took place or may take place, past, present, or future, or when the imagined incident was fantasied, or when the crucial situation out of which this present enactment arose, occurred." Moreno had observed that it was almost impossible to recall and re-enact a scene that had occurred five minutes earlier with the same actors. He asserted that speaking in the past tense removes the subjects from the immediacy of the experience. He would enjoin his protagonist to "act as if this is happening to you now . . . as if this were happening to you for the first time."

(3) *Subjectivity* "The subject must act out 'his truth,' as he feels and perceives it, in a completely subjective manner (no matter how distorted this appears to the spectator)." Patients must be accepted with all their subjectivity and given the satisfaction of act completion before considering retraining or behavior changes.

(4) *Maximal expression* "The patient is encouraged to maximize all expression, action, and verbal communication, rather than reduce it." Delusions, hallucinations, soliloquies, thoughts, fantasies, projections are all allowed to be part of the production. Restraint may come after the expression.

(5) *Inward movement* "The warming up process proceeds from the periphery to the center." Rather than begin with the most traumatic events, the director should begin at a more superficial level, allowing the involvement of the patient to carry him deeply towards the core.

(6) *Patient choice* "Whenever possible, the protagonist will pick the time, the place, the scene, the auxiliary ego he requires in the production of his psychodrama." The director is there to assist the protagonist in his drama. However, should the interaction between the protagonist and the director become negative, when the protagonist is resisting the director as well as the process, Moreno lists a number of moves the director may make. The possibilities range from asking the patient to choose another director, through asking the patient to choose another scene, to insisting upon the

enactment as the benefits to be derived are greater than maintaining resistance.

(7) *Restraint* "Psychodrama is just as much a method of restraint as it is a method of expression." Although psychodrama allows expression in contrast to the repressiveness of everyday life, it also requires restraint on the part of the protagonist who is asked to reverse roles or to enact roles which require retraining or the reconditioning of excitability.

(8) *Acceptance of inexpressiveness* "The patient is permitted to be as unspontaneous or inexpressive as he is at this time." If the patient is unable to express feelings, this must be accepted. Some release may be obtained through asides or soliloquies, the use of a double, or role reversal with some other person or object.

(9) *Interpretation* "Interpretation and insight-giving in psychodrama is of a different nature from the verbal types of psychotherapy." The protagonist may achieve insight from the action in the drama. Directors act upon their interpretations in the construction of scenes. Verbal interpretation may be essential or entirely omitted.

(10) *Action is primary* "Even when interpretation is given, action is primary. There can be no interpretation without previous action." Interpretation may be questioned, rejected, or totally ineffective. The action speaks for itself. At times, interpretation may be destructive. What the patient may require is not analysis, but emotional identification.

(11) *Cultural adaptations* "Warming up to psychodrama may proceed differently from culture to culture and appropriate changes in the application of the method have to be made." In some cultures, one may need to start with singing and dancing; in others, this would be inappropriate. "The important thing is not how to begin but that we begin."

(12) *Three-part procedure* "Psychodrama consists of three portions: the warm up, the action portion and the post-action sharing by the group." Disturbances in any of these phases may reflect on the total process. Sharing need not be verbal. It could be a pregnant silence, or having group members carry out some activity together.

(13) *Identification with protagonist* "The protagonist should never be left with the impression that he is all alone with this type of problem in this group." If in the post-action phase the directors cannot draw from the group some identifications with the subjects, then it is the task of the directors to reveal themselves as not merely being in sympathy with the protagonist, but as having similar problems. This may warm up others in the audience to make disclosures.

(14) *Role playing*   "The protagonist must learn to take the role of all those with whom he is meaningfully related, to experience those persons in his social atom, their relationship to him and to one another." The patient must learn to "become" any person or object that is significant in order to overcome distortions and manifestations of imbalance in the relationships and to re-integrate them on a new level. Role reversal allows a patient to grow beyond experiences that have a negative impact and become more spontaneous along positive lines.

(15) *Flexibility*   "The director must trust the psychodrama method as the final arbiter and guide in the therapeutic process." When the warm up of the director is objective, spontaneous, and available to the needs of the patient and group, then the psychodramatic method will lead systematically to the heart of the patient's suffering. The director, patient, auxiliaries, and group members become a cohesive force to maximize emotional learning.

Techniques

Zerka Moreno's list of "techniques" (Moreno and Moreno, 1969: 239–44) can be divided into two categories: those that are used in the course of a psychodrama, which will be presented first, and those that constitute special forms of psychodrama, which are described in the next section of the chapter. In the first category are six techniques: soliloquy, therapeutic soliloquy, double, multiple double, mirror, and role reversal. Treadwell et al. (1990) list some 44 variations of these techniques.

(1) *Soliloquy*   A monologue by the protagonist as if in conversation with the audience.

(2) *Therapeutic soliloquy*   The portrayal, by side thoughts and side actions, of hidden thoughts and feelings that parallel overt thoughts and actions.

(3) *Double*   The patient portrays himself or herself, while an auxiliary ego is asked to "establish identity with the patient" and to act like the patient, saying or doing things the auxiliary feels that the patient might want to say or do, subject to correction by the patient.

(4) *Multiple double*   The patient is on the stage with several doubles, each playing some part of himself or herself. For example, one double may be acting and reacting as the patient was in the past, another as the patient is in the present, and another as the patient might be in the future.

(5) *Mirror*   When the patient is unable to represent himself or herself, in word and action, an auxiliary ego represents him or her

on the stage while the patient watches from the audience. The auxiliary ego acts to show the patient "as if in a mirror" how other people experience him/her. The auxiliary may exaggerate actions in order to arouse the patient to come to the stage to make corrections and become an active participant.

(6) *Role-reversal* The patient is asked to "step into the shoes" of another person, who may be a real person or an auxiliary acting the part, while the other person assumes the patient's role. In this way, distortions of interpersonal perception can be brought to the surface and corrected.

Special forms of psychodrama

The special forms of psychodrama that Moreno used are self-presentation, self-realization, hallucinatory psychodrama, future projection, dream presentation, retraining of the dream, and a therapeutic community. Following generations of psychodramatists added more special forms to this list; for example, the "magic shop" in which the protagonist enters a shop to trade some undesired quality for a new one.

(1) *Self-presentation* The protagonist presents himself or herself, members of his family, or others who have a significant relationship. This form is often used as an introduction to a new group.

(2) *Self-realization* The protagonist, with the help of auxiliaries, enacts the ideal plan for his or her life, no matter how remote from the present. Alternatives may be explored, such as the success of a new venture, possible failure, or the return to an old livelihood.

(3) *Hallucinatory psychodrama* The patient enacts the hallucinations and delusions that he or she is presently experiencing. Auxiliaries take the parts of voices, visions, or other phenomena to involve the patient in interaction with them, so as to put them to a reality test.

(4) *Future projection* The patient portrays in action some situation that he or she expects to be involved with in the future, including the place and the people. This is a version of self-realization, but with a focus on a particular future event.

(5) *Dream presentation* The patient enacts a dream. After warming up to the setting, the patient is asked to lie down and relax as if in sleep. As the dream is recalled, the patient, with the help of auxiliaries, acts out the dream. An example of this form was given earlier in this chapter.

(6) *Retraining of the dream* After enacting a dream, the patient is asked to change the dream, to act, with the help of auxiliaries, a preferred situation, thus to retrain the dreamer rather than interpret.

(7) *Therapeutic community*   In Moreno's words, "This is a community in which disputes and conflicts between individuals and groups are settled under the rule of therapy instead of the rule of law. The entire population, patients and staff alike, are responsible for the welfare of every other person, participate in the therapeutic process and have equal status." This is clearly more than simply another form of focus of a psychodrama. Perhaps Moreno saw his sanatorium at Beacon, where patients and staff lived on the same premises and joined in the same psychodramas, as an instance of a therapeutic community.

Adjunctive methods

Adjunctive methods are those in which some other form or focus of intervention is combined with psychodrama. Moreno's list includes hypnodrama, psychodramatic shock, improvisation for personality assessment, didactic psychodrama and role playing, psychodrama combined with narcosynthesis, LSD, etc., and family psychodrama and family therapy.

(1) *Hypnodrama*   After being hypnotized, the patient is free to move about and is provided with auxiliaries to help portray his drama. Moreno and Enneis (1950) provide a description of hypnodramatic techniques.

(2) *Psychodramatic shock*   Patients are asked to throw themselves back into the hallucinatory experience. If they are fearful and resistant, the director explains that the purpose is to learn control, not mere re-living, and that this enactment will help them build resources against recurrence.

(3) *Improvisation for personality assessment*   With the help of auxiliaries, the director stages a situation from life and asks the subject to react as if it were actually happening to him or her. This provides a profile of the action potential of the individual. Moreno used this type of assessment in his work at the Hudson School. Some examples are given later in the chapter.

(4) *Didactic psychodrama and role playing*   As a teaching method, professionals are asked to take the role of the client and also their own role in enactments of typical conflicts that occur in the process of treatment in their profession.

(5) *Psychodrama combined with narcosynthesis, LSD, etc.*   Under the influence of drugs, the patient re-lives certain experiences. If patients have already undergone drug therapy, they may act out their inner experiences that they were unable to communicate while under the influence of the drug.

(6) *Family psychodrama and family therapy* Family members are treated in the same session where they may be asked to reverse roles, double for each other, or serve as each other's auxiliary ego.

The director and auxiliary egos as social investigators

In an article written with Dunkin (Moreno and Dunkin, 1941; see also Moreno, 1972: 252–61), Moreno described the functions of the director and auxiliary egos as social investigators. Moreno begins with the assertion:

> The experimental psychodrama has shown that controlled experiments in the social sciences can be carried out – for the first time, it is believed, in the evolution of the social sciences – with the same precision as in the so-called natural sciences. More particularly, it is possible to make the social investigator, who is inside the social situation, an objective part of the material studied – to have him, so to speak, both inside the experiment and outside of it. What has hitherto been, in the strict sense, impossible, now becomes possible: man can be his own "guinea-pig."
> (Moreno and Dunkin, 1941: 392)

Moreno would begin the exploration of a social problem with an exploration of the social investigator. Moreno would use psychodrama to explore the investigator's role and what he is thinking before, during, and after the investigation. When psychodrama is the method of investigation for a social problem, then it is the director who should be analyzed as the social investigator. In addition to the director's approach to a particular case, there are general functions that a director fills in each psychodrama. These general functions are the subject of Moreno's article.

In relation to the protagonist and the stage, Moreno would take three different positions, each associated with one of the directorial functions: the interview, observer, and spectator positions. One can see him in action in his description of the three different positions.

(1) *Interview position* The director is sitting on the second level of the stage at the center point. He is relaxed, perhaps his elbow rests on the upper level of the stage where the action will take place and his feet rest comfortably on the first level. In this way, the director does not dominate the audience. When he calls upon the protagonist to sit beside him for the initial interview, they are as equals. However, Moreno notes that with other stage designs or other action areas, different positions would be used. The director returns to this central position at the end of every scene for analysis or to warm up a subject for the following scene. Whether the subject sits on the right or left of the director is a matter of choice.

(2) *Observer position* The director stands on the audience level at the right of the stage, close to the wall. This gives the director a close view of the stage and a full view of the audience. The director may place his right foot on the lowest level of the stage so that he can lean forward for close observation or step up on to the stage if some intervention is required.

(3) *Spectator position* In this position the director is sitting in the front row, somewhat removed from active participation in the action on stage. He may call upon a resisting subject to sit beside him to warm up while a pertinent scene is taking place on the stage.

Moreno warns directors that they should avoid rigidly adhering to these positions but to adapt their positions and movements to the situation.

People who are called upon to act auxiliary egos should observe what the role does to them and what they do to it. They should be observing participants. For auxiliaries, empathy with the role is not enough. Auxiliaries in action are not only feeling but doing; they are both constructing and reconstructing present or absentee subjects. Auxiliaries as social investigators study the subjects by becoming the subjects.

The director can discover the range of roles that an auxiliary may play by the use of spontaneity tests (see the descriptions of tests in the account of research at the Hudson School below). Auxiliaries play three types of role: a real person who is related to the subject, an imaginary character, or a part of the subject's own ego. "The proof of his success is the subject's acceptance of him in the role."

Applications of psychodrama

Psychodrama, in whole or through the use of some of its techniques, was and is used in a variety of settings and with a broad spectrum of target populations. Many of the applications were foreshadowed by Moreno's own early work with psychotics, the treatment of marital problems, people with alcohol and substance abuse problems, the field of corrections, and prison populations. For example, in the mental health field, applications range from psychodrama programs in in-patient psychiatric facilities to the use of specific techniques in private practice with individuals, couples, families, or groups. Moreno maintained that there was no classification of psychosis nor, indeed, any problems that are not amenable to treatment by psychodrama under certain conditions.

Bruch (1954) reports the effective use of psychodrama by a therapist in a clinical setting to free an eight-year-old child from severe tics and partial paralysis of his upper right arm. Tom had developed the tic just after receiving an injection in his arm for a "TB scratch test" at school. In the psychodrama, Tom played the part of the doctor giving the injections and the director, as an auxiliary, played the parts of several boys who were anxious about the injections. By the end of the session, after Tom had verbalized his anxieties and his fear of being taunted by the "toughies" at the school, his symptoms had disappeared.

Sasson (1990) describes the use of psychodrama with adolescents at a treatment center that had both residential and outpatient treatment programs for patients with conditions ranging from mild to severe psychiatric illness. Additional articles in a special issue of the *Journal of Group Psychotherapy, Psychodrama and Sociometry* (1990, vol. 43, no. 3) provide examples of work with adolescents in other settings. Another special issue (1990, vol. 43, no. 2) includes examples from university education.

Blatner's summary of the contribution of psychodrama to practice is as follows (Blatner and Blatner, 1988: 87–8):

> It is an approach that supports and is supported by the growing trend toward eclecticism in psychotherapy. . . . Activity and the use of techniques that increase the vividness of the experience add to the empowerment of the patient. Including a skill building orientation addresses deeper attitudes while sustaining the cognitive elements of the therapeutic alliance. Developing channels of self-expression helps generate healthy sublimations for previously uncultivated emotional needs. Emphasizing the future and applying methods for developing the capacity to create a more vigorous ego ideal is another important aspect of therapy. In all of these, the patients are helped to make more functional bridges between their subjective experiences and objective assessments of reality. These components offer significant additions to the range of therapeutic interventions and are thus relevant to the challenge of healing.

Moreno saw psychodrama and group therapy as two independent developments. Both sociometry and group psychotherapy are nested in a network of interpersonal relations as revealed by sociometry. Group psychotherapy represented the science of the group and psychodrama the science of action. Moreno designated sociometry, group psychotherapy, and psychodrama as the "triadic system" (Moreno, 1970). However, psychodrama is the broader classification since verbal group psychotherapy is then, in effect, the audience portion of a psychodrama without the action portion. Moreno observed that many group psychotherapists tended to rely on analysis and interpretation or discussion and verbal confrontation. He asserted that a major contribution of psychodrama was to insist that "even verbal interchange should not be of this nature, but more on the basis of an encounter, with group members sharing revelations about themselves rather than analyzing and interpreting" (1973: 24). Not only was sharing beneficial for the protagonist by providing support, but it also prepared members of the audience for the next step by warming them up for becoming protagonists themselves.

Moreno's sociometric study at the Hudson School for Girls

The review by Hare (1992) of Moreno's work of sociometric reconstruction of the community at the New York Training School for Girls from 1932 through 1938 is reproduced in the following account. In *Who Shall Survive?* (1953), Moreno describes his Sociometric Tests of home and work groups, types of sociometric classification, the Acquaintance Test, the Spontaneity Test, the Situation Test, and the Role-playing Test. Procedures are outlined for the construction and reconstruction of the community, including the Parent Test and the Family Test. By the end of the intervention, the amount of attraction between girls in the cottages had increased and the number of girls who ran away from the school had decreased.

Moreno's description of his major sociometric reconstruction of the community at the Hudson School for Girls fills some 300 pages of *Who Shall Survive?* (1953). This summary of Moreno's research is provided as a reminder of the complexity of his program of intervention for those already familiar with the general outlines of his work and as an introduction for those who may become motivated to read the original work in all its detail, including the many sociometric diagrams. Throughout the summary, most of the terms and phrases are Moreno's. However, we have only used quotation marks when it is especially important that the reader be aware of Moreno's exact description of the material.

The Hudson School for Girls provided an opportunity for Moreno to develop and use a number of sociometric techniques and other techniques that deal with interaction in small groups. Although he used some or all of these techniques in other educational or community settings, his work at the Hudson School, between 1932 and 1938, represents his most extensive use of these methods. His aim was to balance the spontaneous social forces "to the greatest possible harmony and unity of all."

For Moreno, the work at the Hudson School was the closest he had come to a complete sociometric experiment. However, he cautioned that one should be aware of how far it was from going the whole way. Its administrative structure was only partly involved. The profit motive and economic dynamics did not enter into the experimental design. The paternalistic character of the community made the experiment comparatively "flat" and "easy." A change in the system of values did not enter the experiment because the desire for such a change was not articulated in the membership. All in all, Moreno concluded, the complete sociometric experiment was still a project for the future.

The New York Training School for Girls, near Hudson, New York, was the size of a small village of between 500 and 600 people. All of the residents were girls who were sent from every part of New York State by the courts and would stay at Hudson for several years until their "training" had been completed. In its organization, the community consisted of two groups: staff members and students. There were 16 cottages where the residents lived, a chapel, a school, a hospital, a small department store, an industrial building, a steam laundry, an administration building, and a farm. The black population was housed in cottages separate from the white. However, in education and in social activities, the girls mixed freely. In each house there was a housemother who had the function of a parent. All meals were cooked in the houses under the direction of a kitchen officer. The girls participated in the houses in different functions, as waitresses, kitchen helpers, laundresses, or corridor girls.

The research at Hudson, as well as that in several other situations, was first reported in *Who Shall Survive?* in 1934. In that edition Moreno collaborated with Helen Jennings who played a major role in the collection and analysis of the data. The material presented here is summarized from the second edition of the book (Moreno, 1953: 219–527).

Moreno wished to know more than the obvious social organization of the community. He observed that whatever the "social structure" of a particular cottage might be, it was necessary to ascertain the psychological function of each of its members and the "psychological organization" of the cottage group. The social function of a girl, for instance, might be that of supervising the dormitory, but her psychological function might be that of the housemother's pet who was rejected by the members of her group and isolated within it.

The social organization of the total community had beneath its outer appearance another aspect. Although separately housed, there were attractions and repulsions between black and white girls that gravely affected the social conduct of the community. The "emotional currents" radiating from white to black girls, and vice versa, had to be ascertained in detail, their causes determined, and their effects estimated. Similarly, emotional currents radiated from one cottage to another among the white population irrespective of their housing and other distinctions. Psychological currents also flowed between the officers and students and between the officers themselves. The sum total of all of these currents affected and shaped the character and conduct of each person and each group in the community.

Moreno was aware that his experiment would not be welcomed equally by all segments of the community (1953: 220–2). Although he had the support of the superintendent, he also had to deal with the Board of Trustees, the staff, and the Department of Social Welfare in the City of Hudson. He sensed that he had friends and enemies in all sections of the population. As a method of measuring his relationship with the various groups, he used a "sociometric self-rating." Two or three times a day, he would map out in his mind his relationships with key groups upon whom the success or failure of the project depended.

Sociometric tests of home groups

The natural family that is the cell of social organization in the community at large was missing at Hudson. The girls were separated from their parents and assigned to a housemother. They were also separated from their siblings and placed in groups of girls who were unrelated to them and to each other. For the natural parent, a "social" parent had been substituted; for the natural child, a "social" child. Moreno used the Sociometric Test (asking individuals with whom they would choose to associate for a given activity) to determine the "drawing power" that one girl had for another or for the housemother, and in return the drawing power of the housemother for a girl. Through this device, he wished to find out to whom each girl was attracted and by whom each girl was repelled. The analysis of the sum total of these attractions and repulsions would give an insight into the distribution of emotions in the community and the position of each individual and group in relation to the emotional currents.

On the Sociometric Test, used at Hudson, the *criterion* toward which the attention of the girls was directed was their liking or disliking of other members of the community with respect to living in the same house as them. At that time the total population of the school from which the girls could select home associates was 505. After pre-tests, Moreno decided that each girl should be allowed five choices to provide sufficient data. The test was given to all the girls at the same time. Moreno always insisted that the criterion of choice should be clear and that the group or community should be reorganized on the basis of the results of the test. In this case the instructions were as follows (1953: 104):

> You live in a certain house with certain other persons according to the directions the administration has given you. The persons who live with you in the same house are not chosen by you and you are not chosen by them, although you might have chosen each other. You are now given the opportunity to choose persons with whom you would like to live in the same house. You can choose without restraint any individuals in this community whether they happen to live in the same house with you or not. Write down whom you would like first best, second best, third best, fourth best, and fifth best. Look around and make up your mind. Remember that the ones you choose will probably be assigned to live with you in the same house.

Each girl was then classified according to the choices she had made and the choices she had received. A drawing was made to represent each girl's "social atom" with large circles to represent other cottages and small circles to represent girls within a cottage that had been chosen by the subject or had chosen her. A choice was represented by a line extending half way from one individual to another. If the choice was positive the line was solid, if negative the line was dashed.

Larger "sociograms" were constructed to illustrate the choices of members of a single cottage. The actual composition of the cottage could then be compared with the composition desired by its members, whom would they like to have in and whom out of the cottage. In a typical cottage, Moreno observed that there were some girls who, like stars, captured most of the choices, others formed mutual pairs, sometimes linked into long mutual chains or into triangles, squares, or circles. Some girls were not chosen.

After drawing sociograms to represent the choices for each cottage, Moreno found that the choices ran criss-cross throughout the total community, uncovering the invisible dynamic organization that actually existed below the official one. Suddenly, what had seemed blank or impenetrable for him opened up as a great vista. The choices ran in streams from one cottage to another. Some cottages concentrated their choices within their own group. Others gave so many choices to other cottages that it appeared that they desired to disband.

Limits of emotional interest

Instead of the 2,525 choices expected on the Sociometric Test, only 2,285 were actually made. Individuals varied in the extent to which they used their choices. Two hundred girls used only four choices and some less. Moreno suggests that the process of slowing down of interest, the cooling off of emotional expansiveness, represents the *sociodynamic decline* of interest. After a certain number of efforts the interest grows fatigued. It reaches extinction of interest in respect to a certain criterion, the sociodynamic limit of a person's expansion, its *social entropy*.

Sociodynamic effect

Another process was observed to occur with a peculiar regularity. The number of choices was not divided equally among the girls. Some attracted more attention, receiving more choices, while some attracted less attention, receiving fewer choices or remaining unchosen. A few girls received more than 40 choices and 75 girls remained unchosen. Moreno called the process of persistently leaving out a number of persons in a group the *sociodynamic effect*.

Attractions, repulsions and indifference

Human relations, Moreno observed, could be compared to a stick with two ends. The emotions going out from a person are only one half of the stick. The emotions coming back are the other half. To provide information concerning the motives for each individual's choices, each girl was interviewed to find out how she felt about living with the persons she had chosen or rejected and what motives she had for choosing or rejecting them. Each person she had indicated was also asked how they would feel about living with her and what motives they had. The set of individuals that interlocked with any given individual Moreno designated the *social atom*. The Sociometric Test was the first attempt to detect these atoms. The interviews attempted to penetrate beneath the surface and determine the motivations for choice. For example, one girl says of her first choice "we seem to understand each other although we are very different." Her first choice declares that she is "so interesting. She seems to feel things so deeply." Moreno did not categorize the motivations by type.

At the Hudson School the 505 atomic structures often differed from the position of the individuals in their home groups. The structures frequently overlapped with one another, with many individuals being part of several structures at the same time.

Sociometric classification

On the basis of the Sociometric Test, Moreno was able to classify each individual and each group within a community. In contrast to methods of classification that were current at the time, Moreno did not classify individuals separately. Rather, he defined an individual in relation to other individuals and a group in relation to other groups. Moreno constructed a table for each individual showing choices sent and received, in or out of the group. In each four cells of the table, the first figure represented attractions and the second (separated by a dash) the rejections. The choices and rejections sent and received inside the group represent an individual's position in the group. The choices and rejections given and received outside the group represent an individual's position in the community.

Moreno identified nine types of sociometric classification. An individual might be classified as belonging to several types (1953: 235):

1 *Positive or negative*: positive, the subject chooses others; negative, the subject does not choose others.

2 *Isolated*: the subject is not chosen and does not choose.

3 *Extroverted position*: the subject sends the majority of her choices to individuals outside her own group.

4 *Introverted position*: the subject sends the majority of her choices to individuals inside her own group.

5 *Attracted*: the subject uses more than half of the choices permitted.

6 *Attractive*: the subject receives more than half of the choices permitted. ("In" or "out" is added to indicate whether the choices are inside the subject's group or outside. When this is not added, the choices are understood to relate to both inside and outside the group.)

7 *Rejecting*: the subject uses more than half of the rejections permitted.

8 *Rejected*: the subject receives more than half of the rejections permitted.

9 *Indifference*: the subject is indifferent to the individuals who are attracted to her or who reject her.

In classifying individuals, Moreno did not rely on sociometric data alone. For example, the classification of one girl as isolated, rejected, and rejecting was corroborated by an intensive study of her conduct, while the negative and isolated situation of another girl in the community was verified by her lack of sociability. In each case, the sociometric classification was substantiated by clinical evidence and further testing. Any change of conduct appeared immediately in the Sociometric Test. When the Sociometric Test showed a change in classification, a change in conduct was evidenced.

Even though two individuals might have the same or a similar sociometric classification, one might be part of a network of individuals who were well adjusted, while the other might be chosen by individuals who are practically cut off from the rest of the community. Thus, Moreno observed that the sociometric position of an individual is not sufficiently defined unless the Sociometric Test is given to the whole community to which that individual belongs. The surrounding structure may throw new light upon the position of an individual and revise a premature interpretation. At the Hudson School, further differentiations between individuals were obtained by studying their relation to their respective house-mothers and their classification in their respective work groups.

Group and community organization

Several measures were derived to provide a basis for classifying types of group and community organization. For the cottage groups, the number of choices going inside the group were compared with those going outside the group. If the majority of group members prefer to remain within the group, then the organization tends to be *introverted*. If the majority of the members want to live outside, then the group tends to be *extroverted*. An introverted group organization tends to be warm and overfilled with emotion. An extroverted group organization tends to be cold, as little emotion is spent within it. When the members are not interested in whom they live with, either with each other or with outsiders, the organization is one of *solitaires*. If the introverted and extroverted tendencies reach an equilibrium, the organization is *balanced*. On average, the members of the cottages at the Hudson School showed more attraction for members inside the cottage than outside. It was evident, therefore, that the cohesive forces at work in the community were stronger than the forces drawing the girls away from their cottage groupings.

Organization of work groups

The first goal of the research had been to analyze the relationships within and between cottage groups. When the research team next applied the Sociometric Test to the work situation, an additional factor had to be considered: the nature of the work, including the materials, tools, and machines. Two aspects now entered the test: (a) the relations of the workers to each other and their supervisor, and (b) the relation of the workers to the particular technological process. A third aspect, the economic, was not evaluated in the test since at the Hudson School monetary compensation was excluded.

The Sociometric Test was varied to fit the new situation and given in the following manner. The tester entered the work room and tried to establish rapport with the group by explaining that sincere answering of questions about to be put to them might lead to a better adjustment of their work situation to their wishes. Each individual was asked:

1 Did you choose the work you are doing now? If not, name the work you would prefer to do.
2 Choose five girls from the community whom you would like best of all as co-workers and name them in order of preference, first choice, second choice, third, fourth, and fifth. The individual you choose may at present be in your home group or in this work group or in other groups. Choose without restraint whomever you prefer to work with.
3 Choose three co-workers from the group in which you are now participating whom you prefer to work with. Name them in order of preference: first choice, second choice, and third choice. Consider in choosing that some parts of the work are done by you in association with a second or third person and you may wish other associates instead of the ones you have now.

The test was given to all work groups in the community. Where incompatible individuals were identified, changes were made in the group composition or organization with a resulting increase in productivity. In the steam laundry, for example, the two girls who had key roles as feeders of the machines were found to reject each other. One of them was the leader of a rebellious gang that had set off a race riot in the school. The two girls who, as catchers, removed the laundry from the machine also rejected each other. When the rebellious girl and one of the catchers was replaced, the relationships between members and with the supervisor were improved. The relationship between the new pair of feeders was indifferent and the relationship between the new pair of catchers was positive. As a result, the output of the whole group improved and interpersonal frictions were much reduced.

In a comparison of home groups with work groups, Moreno noted that a lack of positive choice within a work group may have a less disturbing effect than within a home group. Interest in the work can provide compensation for lack of interest in co-workers.

Acquaintance Test
Once the Sociometric Test had given information about the network of persons who had a fairly strong positive or negative attraction for each other, Moreno became interested in the number of people within each individual's range of social contact. To provide this information, he devised the Acquaintance Test to measure the volume of social expansion of an individual. The test was given to every incoming girl as she arrived; the conditions were

the same for every individual tested; and the test was repeated every 30 days. The instructions were as follows:

> Write the names of all the girls whom you can recall at this moment to have spoken to at any time since you came to Hudson. It does not matter how long ago you made an acquaintance, nor if you spoke to her only once or many times. If you do not recall an acquaintance's full name, write her nickname or her first name or identify the person in some way. Do not include girls with whom you live in your cottage.
> (Moreno, 1953: 287)

From the analysis of the data for 16 girls tested over a six-month period, it is evident that the acquaintance volume varies considerably from individual to individual. Six months after entering the Hudson School, living under the same conditions and having the same opportunity to meet others, one individual had only eight acquaintances while another had 131. The first girl had her acquaintances distributed among five cottages, whereas the second had hers distributed among 16 cottages. Although the number of acquaintances showed some relation to a girl's intelligence, it was more closely related to her social and emotional skills.

Spontaneity Test

After analyzing the sociometric network and the motivation of the members of a group, Moreno found that he wished to go deeper into the structure of the group. He wanted to devise a way to watch how individuals enter into social relations. He felt that arousing and probing the spontaneity of the individual was the alpha and omega of the search.

As an example of the Spontaneity Test, Moreno presents the case of Elsa who was one of a group of five in her cottage of 25 girls. Elsa was classified on the basis of the Sociometric Test as isolated and rejected. The data from the motivation test supported this classification.

The purpose of the Spontaneity Test is to explore the range and intensity of the spontaneity of individuals in their exchange of emotions. Moreno would observe a subject in spontaneous interaction with another person in the test situation. He would also observe the type and volume of the emotions of the others and the spontaneous reaction of each of them toward the subject. A subject was instructed as follows:

> Throw yourself into a state of emotion towards X. The precipitating emotion may be either anger, fear, sympathy, or dominance. Develop any situation you like to produce with her, expressing this particular emotion, adding to it anything which is sincerely felt by you at this time. Throw yourself into the state with nothing on your mind but the person

who is opposite you. *Think of this person as the real person whom you know so well in everyday life. Call her by her actual name and act towards her the way you usually do.* Once you have started to produce one of these emotional states, try to elaborate the relations towards that person throughout the situation, living out any experience, emotional, intellectual, or social. (Moreno, 1953: 347)

The partner receives no instructions except to react as she would in actual life to the attitude expressed toward her by the subject. The two persons are *not allowed* to consult with each other before they begin to act.

Moreno observes that this type of Spontaneity Test is not entirely unstructured because the two partners operating in the situation know one another. Life has already prepared them for each other and for the test. They do not need any preparation as to their feelings for each other and the kind of conflicts they get into. This is different from the psychodramatic situation test in which the subject faces an auxiliary ego who is an artificial experimental agent.

In the course of the test, the person tested is placed opposite every person who is found to be related to her. After the subject has produced any one of the four states toward a partner (either anger, fear, sympathy, or dominance), the partner is instructed to produce the state she chooses toward the subject. The person tested may choose to produce the same state toward all partners, for instance, sympathy, or she may produce a different state each time. She may start out to be cordial and sympathetic but before she knows it her true feeling will show and she warms up to anger and hostility.

The reaction time, the words spoken, the mimic expression, and the movements in space of both individuals are recorded by the tester. Every ten seconds the number of words spoken is recorded. The interaction pattern for each individual is symbolized along a time line of alternating periods of interaction and pauses, with the number of words spoken during each period of interaction indicated (1953: 361–2).

Situation Test and Role-playing Test

According to plan, Moreno moved with his research into further dimensions of group structure. The Situation Test was designed to explore the "situation matrix," consisting of space and time relations, locus and movements, acts and pauses, volume of words and gestures, initiation, transfer, and termination of scenes. The Role-playing Test was designed to explore the "role matrix" of a group that consists of private and social roles.

As an illustration, Moreno describes the activities of Elsa who took part in one of the role-playing groups that were organized for test purposes. She was often given the occasion to act out different roles, such as the role of a daughter or a mother, a girlfriend or a sweetheart, a housemaid or a wealthy lady, a pickpocket or a judge. She acted these parts in a great variety of life situations as they had impressed themselves upon her while growing up as an adolescent in the slums of a great industrial city. In one of these situations she is faced with a home conflict in which mother and father have a heated argument that finally leads to their separation. In another situation, she is faced with a work conflict in which she gets fired from a job because she comes in late. A third situation presents a love conflict in which she loves a boy who is as poor and rejected as she is.

An analysis of the text and gestures produced in these role-playing situations gave Moreno clues to understand Elsa's early family life better and the emotional tensions that gradually brought about her present status. The role plays also gave those members of the group who rejected her an opportunity to see Elsa operate in a variety of situations other than those to which they were accustomed.

In the pages of *Who Shall Survive?* Moreno provides a detailed analysis of the data drawn from the Spontaneity Test and the Situation and Role-playing Tests. He finds that what may appear on the surface as an attraction or rejection may actually be a complex mix of emotions. In Elsa's case, he found that the network that contributed to her conflict was so widely spread that a spontaneous adjustment had become almost impossible for her to attain. An attempt at a cure involved a whole chain of individuals with whom her position was interlocked. A transfer was arranged to another cottage where it might be possible for her to establish new relationships with the girls and with the housemother.

Further sociometric analysis

Moreno continued his sociometric analysis of aspects of community life with studies of the extent to which the cottage provided a "psychological home" for the girls, the network surrounding two girls who ran away, and the effect of having members of two "races" and only one gender in the community.

As a method for the analysis of the sociometric data for the whole community, Moreno made maps of the "psychological geography." A map shows the topographical layout of the Hudson School and the psychological currents relating each region within it to each other region. Red lines from one cottage to another represent currents of attraction, black lines currents of repulsion, and lines that are half red and half black represent split currents.

The maps demonstrate a trend of greater friendliness toward cottages and neighborhoods that are more distantly located and a trend of greater incompatibility with adjacent groups. Being neighbors, it appears, gives more occasion for friction to arise as contacts are more frequent and intimate. It would seem that what is present and helpful is often forgotten by neighbors and what is unpleasant turns them away to look into the distance. Exceptions to the rule are two cottages that are so far removed from the rest that they are more dependent upon each other. They develop more as a single family living in two houses as the attitude of the two housemothers is conciliatory.

The inter-racial relations of the white and black groups make another exception. Here the trend appears to be just the opposite of the above. The closer the white cottages are to the black, the friendlier is the attitude between them. The further the white cottages are from the black, the less interested are both sides.[2]

An analysis of the data on girls who ran away from the school over a two-year period indicated that girls who ran away lived in cottages ranked among the lowest for interest in living with members of the cottage, i.e. the most "extroverted" cottages. These cottages also tended to have a high number of incompatible pairs. Moreno concludes that it is always the organization of the group that keeps an individual within the fold or forces the individual out.

Moreno continued to look in detail at the various types of relationships revealed in the sociometric data. In *Who Shall Survive?* he suggests how one might construct sociometric indices of these relationships that might provide clues to the possibility of intervention using group psychotherapy, psychodrama, role playing, or sociodrama (1953: 452–5).

Construction and reconstruction of the community
Once Moreno had a grasp of the sociometric structure of the community, he set about the task of constructing compatible households as new girls entered the community, and reconstructing old households and work groups as problems became evident. As an aid to construction, Moreno devised two more tests, the Parent Test (1953: 463–4), which allowed him to identify compatible pairs of girls and houseparents, and the Family Test (1953: 470–1), which allowed him to identify a cottage that would welcome each new girl.

For the Parent Test, each new girl was asked to entertain in her room in the reception cottage each of the housemothers who had a vacancy in their cottages. After the series of interviews, the girls and the housemothers were asked about their choices and their motivations for choices. The testing continued with the Family Test. The procedure was similar, only this time the new girl talked to a girl, selected by the housemother, who represented the general tone of the cottage. A different girl represented a cottage at each Family Test.[3]

After completing the Parent Test and the Family Test for a new girl, Moreno would go over the cottage organization for each potential assignment. A girl might be placed immediately or she might be asked to remain in the Reception Cottage until the next test if no compatible situation could be found.

Entrance Test: role playing
For the new girl, the tests were not yet over. She still had to go through an Entrance Test and, at the end of her stay at Hudson, an Exit Test. If her initial assignments to a cottage and work group did not prove satisfactory, she would go through a whole battery of tests again.

The Entrance Test consisted of three situations: family, work, and community. In each of these situations, newcomers would enact crucial roles from their daily life, such as daughter, sister, co-worker, wife or girlfriend, churchgoer, and student. The house-mother and key members of the cottage took part in the role plays with them. A jury was present to rate their performances. The role playing gave Moreno decisive clues for the most advantageous assignment for the newcomer.

Total effect of sociometric reconstruction
Within a period of 18 months, 102 individuals, about one-fifth of the population of the school, had been initially assigned to a cottage or re-assigned from one cottage to another. At the end of this period, the status of each cottage group had changed considerably compared with the status it had shown before Moreno began his program of sociometric reconstruction.

A single case of initial assignment would actually involve many more individuals. For example, when 20 new girls were assigned to cottages, more than 200 individuals were in some way involved when one takes into consideration the social atoms, the volume of acquaintance, and the position in the networks of each of these 20 individuals. Moreno presents tables of data to show that the ratio of interest increased in 15 cottages and decreased in one. The average ratio of interest increased by about 10 percent. The sum of attractions, expressed in percentages, increased in 12 cottages and decreased in three. The index of group attraction increased for four cottages, decreased for ten, and remained the same for two.

The best criterion for measuring the adjustment of individuals in a community like the Hudson School, Moreno indicated, was the number of girls who ran away. He felt that the runaway status of the community was an indicator of the extent to which the community had become a psychological home for its members. He knew of few state institutions where the number of runaways was as low as it was at Hudson before the sociometric study, yet there was a remarkable drop in runaway incidents during the years of the study.

The initial assignments through sociometric techniques had begun on 22 February 1933. After a period of four months, the effect of the assignments became evident within the community. The number of runaways gradually dropped. During the following eight months, the number of runaways was unprecedentedly low, a total of six. This would be equally unusual for an open population outside the institution, consisting of an equal number of adolescents. As no essential change in the set-up of the community had been made during this period, either in personnel or in the general character of the population received, the greater inclination of the girls to remain at Hudson could be ascribed to the procedure of assignment. Moreno concluded that a greater number had reached the minimum of adjustment; they did not run away.

Notes

1 Zerka Moreno (personal communication, 1995), who was present at this sociodrama, provides some background to the attitudes of white people toward African-Americans in the 1940s. At the West Coast university where the sociodrama was conducted it was assumed that there was no racial prejudice. Yet, in an interview before the session, the protagonists had indicated that they had experienced a problem finding a place to rent during their study period due to their race. Zerka wondered at the time why Moreno did not deal with the issue more directly with the audience. She guessed that perhaps, as a guest presenter, he felt that this would be too explosive a way of confronting the group. Since Moreno, at times, was very daring in his approaches, Zerka was puzzled. However, she was just an apprentice and felt that she did not have the right or audacity to confront him. In those days an African-American could not stop at a luncheon counter in a white establishment for a drink or a snack or eat in a restaurant and be served civilly. Thus, Zerka suggests that the incidents in the sociodrama were probably eye-openers for white Northerners at the session. She recalls a remark made by Mr Cowley, that when playing chess with a friend, he said: "Isn't it remarkable that in this country black always means something bad? Yet here are equal pieces, both black and white."

2 Zerka Moreno (personal communication, 1995) adds that the two black cottages showed a tremendous number of choices, both positive and negative, within and between the two houses. She sees this as an indication of how racial isolation increased emotional tensions and turned the cottages centripetal.

3 The Family Test sometimes involved a girl who was a sociometric star who helped choose the newcomer. This in itself aided the integration into the cottage of the newcomer. In contrast, when a housemother had a "pet girl" who was a sociometric isolate, and she was involved in the choice of the newcomer, that newcomer's lot was often extremely difficult (Zerka Moreno, personal communication, 1995).

4

Criticism and Rebuttals

In common with other originators of therapeutic techniques, while Moreno was alive it was sometimes difficult to distinguish the inventor's own personal style from the technique he had invented. Moreno gave no evidence of having low self-esteem: he was always ready to promote his own point of view. Thus, the literature includes criticism of both the man and his work. Anthony (1971: 16), reviewing the history of group psychotherapy, cited Moreno's sociometry as "a genuine contribution to social psychology" but, with regard to psychodrama, observed that "to many group therapists he represents a detrimental influence that has split the group world in two, seducing many a group therapist from the careful and patient practice of classical group psychotherapy and leading him into wildly exciting, highly controversial, short-cut methods of treatment."

Moreno sought to provide rebuttals for criticisms of his work. In the "final word," in the prelude to his revision of *Who Shall Survive?* (1953: cviii), he observed: "There is no controversy about my ideas, they are universally accepted. I am the controversy."

We begin this collection of criticisms and rebuttals by noting criticisms of Moreno's theory. Next, we cite the ten most commonly held reservations about psychodrama as compiled by Blatner (1968), as well as additional criticisms that amplify or extend Blatner's list. Criticisms of sociometry and a summary of "lectures" given by Moreno follow, with a final section on criticisms of Moreno's style of writing.

Criticisms of Moreno's theory

As a social scientist, Moreno read the work of the major figures of his day to see how they might support his own ideas, had applied his methods in education, industry, and the armed forces, or more probably had overlooked some basic fact of social life that Moreno had observed (1956: 15–35). Thus he includes discussion of the work of Mead (1947b; also 1951b: 119–22), Homans, Marx (1949b; also 1951b: 159–69), Comte and Freud (1945b).

In his journal articles, Moreno took pains to point out occasions where his contemporaries had misinterpreted him or misquoted him. He felt that Shils had misunderstood his analysis of the primary group, that Gurvitch and von Wiese failed to grasp his assertion that emotions were only one factor in interpersonal choice, that Zaniecki's conclusion that a "cultural conserve" was fixed and stereotyped overlooked the fact that he said it could be vitalized (1956: 29–34). When Gurvitch pointed out inconsistencies in the use of terms, Moreno replied that "certain inconsistencies in the definition of terms are unavoidable in a growing young science, rigidity of definition is perhaps a greater sin" (1956: 34). On another occasion, Gurvitch suggested that Moreno did not recognize the reality of social groups but only dealt with interpersonal relations. Moreno in response agreed that social groups are a reality: "This is in accord with my writings" (1956: 246). Von Wiese also suggested that more emphasis should be placed on the functions, task, and goals of groups, which have more influence on behavior than the networks of interpersonal choice (von Wiese, 1949: 209). When Gurvitch suggested that Moreno should pay more attention to three degrees of interpersonal relationship (mass, community, and communion), Moreno replied: "I am glad to admit that a great many investigations have been outside of my opportunities but at no time have been out of my vision" (Moreno, 1949a: 236).

Sorokin noted that people have "creative moments" when they formulate a new scientific or technological invention. However, there may have been a long period of trial and error before the inspiration comes. Thus Moreno's Spontaneity Test may not allow enough time to indicate a person's creative potential. Sorokin adds that some of the important instances of creativity in science and the arts were not recognized during the life of the creator. Further, Sorokin suggests that spontaneity–creativity is not energy but "a condition – a conditioning of the subject for free action" (1949: 223). He suggests that Moreno's theory needs clarification and improvement. Sorokin comments again in 1955 on Moreno's summary of his theory of spontaneity–creativity (Moreno, 1955e) and Moreno replies (1955b), describing how he was "warmed up" to reply and reasserting his position.

Moreno focuses on creativity at the moment of an interpersonal encounter, although he uses larger instances of creativity, such as Beethoven's Ninth Symphony, as examples. Sorokin's focus on freedom of action is a reminder that all of the factors identified in social psychology that lead to conformity of action are the opposite of those that lead to creativity (Hare, 1982: 157–8). Thus an individual surrounded by a social atom composed of conformists could not expect to be creative. Since Moreno was only interested in enhancing creativity, in common with many social psychologists, he did not consider the other side of the coin, the factors leading to conformity.

Criticisms of psychodrama

Blatner (1968) lists ten of the most commonly held "reservations" about psychodrama expressed by professionals in psychiatry and related fields and provides rebuttals for each reservation:

1   A fear of *acting out* associated with the meaning of action in psychodrama.
    Rebuttal: "Acting out" is generally conceptualized as an anti-therapeutic discharge of neurotic tensions through behavior which repeats an unconscious situation instead of remembering fully with the appropriate attending emotions. In psycho-drama, the remembering is enacted rather than only verbalized, as in free association. Further, the enactment takes place in the context of group therapy, where the enactment is subject to the observing and analyzing functions of the ego of the protagonist.

2   A fear that enactment may produce overwhelming *anxiety* and *precipitate psychosis* or violent behavior.
    Rebuttal: As in verbal therapies, the problem is not whether to generate anxiety, but rather how to structure this essential process in therapy. The channeling of anxiety is done through the use of proper timing and maintaining coping strategies. Further, a cohesive and confident group can be reassuring to a protagonist who fears loss of control.

3   A criticism that psychodrama seems *unnatural*.
    Rebuttal: All therapies are different from the everyday experi-ence of the patient. Psychotherapy helps a patient re-experience life and interaction in a new light. Although a patient may be more familiar with verbal methods, since this is the norm for the psychoanalytic tradition, once experienced, the richness of the world of action, emotion, and imagination becomes apparent.

4   A concern that psychodrama is *directive*.
    Rebuttal: To be directive by asking the protagonist to try out some activity is not the same as imposing a focus of

investigation or some interpretation upon the patient. The psychodrama director can fully respect the protagonist's choice of a situation to explore even in the most structured of psychodramas.

5   A reservation about the usefulness of *action rather than verbal methods* to clarify group views.

Rebuttal: A group with communication difficulties may not be able to deal with intragroup conflicts by verbal discussion. Often only a shared experience, through the use of action methods, can provide a focus to which all can relate so that different expectations and attitudes can be clarified.

6   A perception of action techniques as *gimmicky*, that the use of "techniques" is incompatible with developing an "honest and genuine relationship" with the patient.

Rebuttal: If the technique is used in an open manner, is explicit, is time limited, and is related to the enactment and not the therapeutic relationship, then the therapist is being neither insincere nor ambiguous.

7   Reservations from persons who have only seen psychodrama being directed by *insufficiently trained* directors when a psychodrama seems boring to the audience or awkward or destructive for the protagonist.

Rebuttal: The problem is not with psychodrama but with the director. A director should use a proper warm up, often involving a great deal of movement. A director should not assign roles to the protagonist which are unfamiliar or too emotionally loaded. A director should ensure a supportive atmosphere in the group, through "sharing" and other methods, otherwise a poorly timed interpretation can lead to a distressing loss of self-esteem for the protagonist.

8   A criticism that regards the involvement of the *use of role as artificial* and that taking a role leads to phoney or game-like behavior.

Rebuttal: The concept of role is compatible with a model of humans as involved, spontaneous, and fully self-actualizing beings.

9   A suspicion that *enactment creates distortion* of the protagonist's conflict, thus rendering the method invalid.

Rebuttal: The same criticism can apply to a verbal therapist since the reconstruction of past events is subject to the censorship of the patient. However, action involves more of the senses in remembering and a greater involvement which reduces defensive maneuvers that distort the revelation of a historical event.

10   Criticism of the *lack of controlled experimental studies* in the field.

Rebuttal: Blatner does not offer a rebuttal; writing in 1968, he agrees that the psychodrama method awaits the validation of properly controlled outcome studies. Ten years later, Kipper (1978) echoed the call for more controlled studies after reviewing 14 research studies in which at least one basic psychodrama technique was used. As we will note below, the same call for research is being made in the 1990s.

Twenty years after compiling his first list of "reservations", Blatner added a few more that focus not so much on the method as on the problems of a therapist using the method (Blatner and Blatner, 1988: 33–7). Therapists accustomed to the "50 minute hour" would be able to treat fewer patients using psychodrama, which requires from two to three hours for a session. If emotions were aroused during a session, more aftercare might be needed. Some therapists, who themselves were introverted and had been trained as passive students, would need to shift to a more active, extroverted role. And, finally, some therapists were put off by Moreno's inclusion of personal, religious, and philosophical themes in his writing, which did not conform to the norm of scientific exposition.

Additional criticisms of psychodrama

Other criticisms can be added to the list, either as new items or as variations of a previous point but with a different emphasis. Kreitler and Elblinger (1961) feel that scenes which could be said to have caused harmful anxiety for the protagonist should be blamed on the anxiety of the therapist or an auxiliary ego. Yablonsky (1968) warns that, since the director is also a group member and participant, the psychodrama setting can create a perfect form for directors who are over-controlling, manipulative, and authoritarian.

Wolson (1971) discusses clinical evidence concerning the danger of precipitating "breakdowns" in psychodrama and the management of loss of impulse control when it does occur. He considers the fear of inducing "psychotic decompensation" in fragile patients the greatest concern among critics of psychodrama. Wolson also notes some of the same criticisms that appear on Blatner's list: lack of clinical expertise and insufficient precautions in selection procedures. Wolson reports that, as a psychodrama director in a psychiatric hospital, he has never seen a patient decompensate or become psychotic in psychodrama. The most dangerous phenomenon he observed was loss of impulse control which occurred in four of the 150 cases he had treated. The impulse that got out of hand was anger. The expressions of anger were abrupt and were managed completely within the psychodrama session.

Wolson concludes that psychodrama with "fragile" patients is relatively safe in the hands of a competent practitioner and offers three case studies to illustrate his point that the actual loss of control may not only occur without harmful effects, but may also provide an opportunity for incisive therapeutic intervention in psychodrama. To maximize the probability of therapeutic results, the director should be attuned to the patient's capacity to tolerate stress and regression, to observe objectively when emotionally upset, and to be responsive to external controls and limit-setting techniques. The staff's ability to control a patient against the patient's will is also important. Wolson concludes with the admonition that in a hospital setting the patients, nursing staff, and doctors must not only view psychodrama as a safe procedure but they must be kept informed of the activity in psychodrama so that there can be a carry-over into the patient's individual therapy and other ward activities.

Writing at about the same time, Moreno (1973) also noted that psychodrama is contraindicated for use with suicidal or homicidal patients, unless precautions are taken to protect the patient from the patient's own actions, and the patient is being seen in the context of a supervised hospital community. Such patients may be so warmed up to enacting in reality that the psychodramatic enactment of fantasies may simply support and prepare the patient to carry out the suicidal or homicidal act in life. Certainly, such enactments are, Moreno felt, contraindicated when working in settings such as day hospitals, offices, or extra-mural clinics.

Moreno (1972: 330) called attention to a special problem that can occur when the psychodrama involves a marriage conflict, especially when there is a third party, another man or woman. He cautions that the situation is so delicate and can cause so much misery and bitterness that the director must take care not to make any suggestion as to which course of action might be preferable. The therapeutic theater is not a court, the auxiliary egos or audience are not a jury, and the director is not a judge. For the director, the best solution to the problem is the one that provides for greater initiative and spontaneity and brings the maximum degree of equilibrium. It may mean the reintegration of the husband–wife pair, or the break-up of the relationship.

Some additional criticisms reinforce Blatner's list. Langley and Langley (1983) also note that training is very important for the psychodrama director. Kellermann (1992: 65) warns that the director should not rely on charisma but on professional competence. Corey (1985) suggests that psychodrama should be used very carefully, if at all, with acting-out individuals. Landy (1986) adds a recommendation for the use of trained auxiliaries rather than relying on members of the group to play supporting roles in a psychodrama. Kellermann (1987) also calls attention to the fact that there is a shortage of rigorous theoretical and empirical research and properly controlled outcome studies of psychodrama. He summarizes 23 studies of "classical" psychodrama, published between 1952 and 1985. He concludes that psychodrama constitutes a valid alternative to other therapeutic approaches, especially in promoting behavior change in adjustment, anti-social, and related disorders. However, he concludes: "the fact that research in psychodrama to this date has had little impact on clinical practice should not discourage future attempts to sub-stantiate its effects by scientific means" (Kellermann, 1987: 467). To this end, Kellermann (1992: 168–72) provides a checklist for processing a psychodrama.

Kane (1992) provides a short list of some of the potential abuses, limitations, and negative effects of classical psychodrama when used in group counseling. She emphasizes the fact that a psychodrama director must have a considerable amount of knowledge, expertise, and practical experience. "In group counseling, the impact of inept, inadequately trained psychodramatists of their inappropriate application of psychodramatic techniques can be harmful to clients, especially to those who are emotionally vulnerable" (Kane, 1992: 181). Her list covers points similar to those of Blatner: the unsuit-ability of some populations, over-controlling directors, inadequately trained auxiliaries. She adds that directors may not spend enough time initially to develop trust and cohesiveness in the group and that sometimes the psychodramatic enactment becomes an end rather than a means in counseling. Her cure for these problems is to conduct more systematic research to explore psychodrama's limitations and abuses.

While waiting for the results of research, Greenberg (1974) would suggest that the best safeguards against improper use of psychodrama and its techniques would be education about the principles involved and an insistence on prescribed approved training for those using the full classical method, since Moreno himself seemed to take it for granted that classical psychodrama would only be practiced by a skilled, trained, director.

The triadic system or concept neutrality?

Some practitioners of psychodrama do not offer direct criticism of Moreno's ideas but rather suggest that it is not necessary to buy the whole package. For example, Kellermann (1987: 77; 1992: 18) questions whether it is necessary to use psychodrama, as Moreno believed, as part of a "triadic system," consisting of sociometry, group psychotherapy and psychodrama. Kellerman sees these as separate methods that may or may not be employed according to the orientation of the practitioner. As a rebuttal, we note that for Moreno the interpersonal network as represented in the social atom is the basic factor in mental health. Thus, without information about an individual's social atom, the therapist and the group acting as therapist will not know where to begin. Psychodrama is a method of investigating an individual's problem through action methods that will provide information for treatment by group therapy. For Moreno, the "triadic system is the integration of three theories: the science of the group, the science of sociometry and the science of action. These are interrelated and indispensable to one another" (Moreno, 1964b: 156).

Kellermann has more to say. In his "Essay on the metascience of psychodrama" (1991), he suggests that most psychodramatists, along with humanistic psychologists, are anti-theoretical, with "a preference for spontaneous action, emotional experience, and release of feelings at the expense of healthy skepticism, critical questioning, and solid research" (Kellermann, 1991: 19). Although Moreno's theories of spontaneity, creativity, the moment, role, and interaction "are useful to explain many clinical situations, they fail to provide a sufficiently uniform and comprehensive theoretical structure for psychodrama therapy" (Kellermann, 1991: 20).

In an earlier article, Kellermann (1987) had proposed a "theory free" procedural definition of psychodrama. Not, he says, because he felt that theory was unnecessary, but because he was trying to unite practitioners of various persuasions within one common framework. Given his definition of psychodrama as a set of procedures for the enactment of a number of scenes, practitioners using a variety of theories, such as psychoanalytic, behavioral, existential, or humanistic could all be said to be conducting psychodramas. Their work need not be based on "psychodramatic" theory. Kellermann's procedural definition is comparable to a definition of psychoanalysis that would include followers of Freud, Klein, Jung, Adler, and others. If psychodrama were only a method, this might work. However, as noted above, if psychodrama, as "social atom repair work," is part of a "triadic system," then only a comprehensive "triadic theory" would provide the necessary basis for its use.

In a response to Kellermann, Kipper (1988) calls attention to his book on clinical role playing in which he proposed a definition of psychodrama and various forms of role playing that would have "a conceptual neutrality" (1986: 24). Earlier, Kipper had also proposed a "procedural definition" of psychodrama as having one or more scenes to present and explore a problem and test solutions (1978: 13). Kipper also felt that "the hitherto claim for an exclusive relationship between the method of psychodrama and Moreno's theory seems unnecessary" (1988: 165). However, a new rationale for the method should be provided. This, Kipper suggests, has not been done by Kellermann, although, as we shall see, Kellermann does make an attempt in his "metascience" article (1991). Kipper proposes a new rationale for psychodrama in the form of a "behavior simulation paradigm" which focuses on an individual's role-playing ability and the possibility of taking corrective measures under simulated conditions. He suggests that psychodrama could be defined as "a method that uses dramatiza-tions of personal experiences through role playing enactments under a variety of simulated conditions as a means for activating psychological processes" (Kipper, 1988: 167). This definition, like Kellermann's "theory free" definition, may tell us what psycho-dramatists do but not why they do it. Moreno had a definite goal in mind, not only to change an individual, on occasion, but concurrently to change the social situation if it was not healthy for the individual.

Returning to "metascience," Kellermann (1991) picks up the ball where he feels Moreno has dropped it. Moreno is credited with a "desperate effort" to create a unified theory of the universe. However, he "attempted to bring together mutually exclusive view points that were often based on contradictory assumptions" (Kellermann, 1991: 20). The "mutually exclusive view points" were not of Moreno's making; they were the familiar natural science versus humanistic science models. For therapy, the first has a goal of symptom removal and adjustment; the second a goal of spontaneity and self-actualization. Although Kellermann finds some evidence for the natural science model in Moreno's writings, he notes that in spite of the quasi-medical language, psychodrama is based on a more humanistic approach. Kellermann suggests an "integrative approach" to reconcile the two views, by adopting behavioral psychodrama with patients who need symptom removal and using existential psychodrama for those who wish to be more liberated from false conceptions about the self and others.

We see no problem with this distinction since the psycho-dramatist would want to start where the patient or protagonist is. Symptom removal may be necessary before the individual can concentrate on more existential issues. Moreno's basic theory is holistic and humanistic. By recreating enactment at "the moment," the patient, therapist, and audience are able to sense the interaction of the social and psychological forces as they interact at one time. However, any description of the process must be done sequentially, thus altering the way in which the situation can be understood. Kellermann's solution for research on psychodrama is to combine both qualitative and quantitative methods in a single study. We are suggesting that even the most qualitative methods of "thick descriptions" have a fundamental drawback in that as they are written down they provide information in a sequential order and not as it occurs in life "at the moment."

Criticisms of sociometry

Criticisms of sociometry, in its limited sense as the measurement of interpersonal choice, are not so much of the method as it was developed by Moreno as of the way it has been adapted and applied in research and action by others. Lindzey and Borgatta (1954), drawing on Moreno's 1934 edition of *Who Shall Survive?* and other early articles, list six rules that should be followed if a Sociometric Test is to be used as Moreno intended:

1 The limits of the group in which the test is given should be indicated.
2 There should be unlimited choices of other persons.
3 Individuals should be asked to choose and reject other group members with a specific criterion or activity in mind.
4 The results of the Sociometric Test should be used to restructure the group; that is, the group should be reorganized by placing people together who have chosen each other as liked.
5 The opinions should be given in private.
6 Questions should be phrased in ways that group members can understand.

In practice, Lindzey and Borgatta estimated that these six rules were followed in only about 25 percent of all sociometric studies. They were writing at a time when the use of sociometry was at its height. The most frequent deviations from the rules were the limitations on choices, usually to about three, and the omission of the step of actually reorganizing the group in line with the results of the test. Some studies also omitted a criterion such as "Who would you choose to work with?" and asked only "Who do you like?" Moreno called this second type of question "near sociometric." At the conclusion of their article, Lindzey and Borgatta describe some "neglected considerations and limitations in the use of sociometric measures" (Lindzey and Borgatta, 1954: 441). These include excessive dependence on sociometric data without considering the more formal aspects of groups and organizations; a scarcity of systematic investigation of the kinds of conditions and variables that are related to sociometric response; insufficient attention to whether the criterion permits one-way or two-way choice; and the treatment of quantitative data without considering the role of chance.

Basic issues of psychotherapy and group psychotherapy

Moreno's presentation of some of the basic issues in psychotherapy and group psychotherapy, and indeed of small groups in general, were given first in a series of lectures in Europe in 1954. He then sent copies of the lectures to 35 colleagues, mainly from the United States, for their comments. The list of colleagues included 17 psychiatrists, ten psychologists, six sociologists, and two theologians. The lectures and the responses of some of the readers were then published in issues of two of Moreno's journals and collected in book form in *Psychodrama, Second Volume: Foundations of Psychotherapy* (Moreno and Moreno, 1959). Moreno notes that in the course of the lectures several contemporary schools of thought are confronted, including existentialism, psychoanalysis, group psychotherapy, communism, and automation.

As an introduction to the series of lectures, Moreno observes that most of the first generation of those who developed methods for individual psychotherapy were gone and most of the protagonists of group and action methods were getting old. Moreno sought to find the common denominators so that the various methods could be brought into a single, comprehensive system. In the meantime, Moreno suggests that each of the current methods, whether the therapist chooses to use a couch, chair, or stage as a setting, could be used according to the needs of the patient.

Lecture 1: Transference, counter-transference and tele:
their relation to group research and group psychotherapy
Freud had observed that a patient projects some unrealistic fantasies upon the therapist. Freud called this "transference." Later, Freud

discovered that therapists were not free from personal involvement with the patient by projecting their own unconscious feelings. Freud called this "counter-transference." For Moreno, there is no "counter." Transference goes both ways as an interpersonal phenomenon. Although there may be some initial transference on both sides, as patient and therapist learn more about each other they are able to form an image of how the other person actually is. This process of mutual appreciation and understanding Moreno called "*tele*." He likened it to a telephone with two ends that facilitates two-way communication. The stability of the therapeutic relationship depends upon the strength of the *tele* between the two participants. The therapist–patient relationship is only an instance of a universal phenomenon that applies to all relationships.

Transference does not take place toward a generalized person or a vague image, but toward the "role" that the therapist presents to the patient. The role may be that of father, mother, wise man, lover, or any other role that is familiar to the patient. The therapist in turn may experience the patient in complementary roles. All individuals have a set of roles and counter-roles with which they are familiar. (On other occasions, Moreno referred to the sets of roles that an individual plays at one time as "cultural atoms.") Each person in the encounter is familiar with how others "look" and "act" when playing these roles.

If the concept of transference is not adequate to explain the relationship between two individuals, it is even less adequate to explain the relationships in group therapy. In a group, the physician can become the patient and the patient a physician. Any member of the group can become the therapist for any other. One must distinguish between the "conductor" of a session and the "therapeutic agents." The wise therapist will eliminate direct face-to-face rapport with the patient and work through other individuals who are in a better position to help. Using the group method, the therapeutic agent may be anyone or a combination of several individuals.

Members' perceptions of their sociometric status are related to their transference behavior. For example, patients who under-evaluate their sociometric status – that is, the number of choices they receive – will tend to rate other members of the group as superior to themselves. *Tele* leads to more accurate perceptions and transference to less accurate perceptions.

To test hypotheses derived from these definitions of transference, *tele*, social perception, role relations, and other concepts related to group psychotherapy, Moreno recommends the use of role-playing techniques. These permit greater flexibility than the observation of actual therapeutic sessions since many versions can be played out with the possibility of using control studies.

Discussion of the lecture comprises 22 pages of text. The name of each discussant is given, followed by his or her comments. Since each discussant read the lecture independently, there is considerable overlap of comment. Some wrote a few paragraphs, others a few pages. Here we reproduce some of the comments by some of the discussants as examples of the main issues that were raised. (Within the quotations the italics and quotation marks are given as in the original text.)

Gordon W. Allport: Dr Moreno defines *tele* as "insight into," "appreciation of," and "feeling for" the "actual makeup" of the other person. Thus defined it is indeed the foundation of all sound therapy, as it is of all wholesome human relationships. [It is also necessary to understand the *social role* of the other person.] If I am challenging Dr Moreno at all, it is merely in connection with his tendency to underestimate the intrinsic difference between the patient's and the therapist's prescribed social roles and frames of mind. *Tele*, as a basis for psychotherapy, should seek to establish appreciation for both the "make up" of personality and for the formal situation that exists by social prescription.

Jules H. Masserman: Moreno's efforts to call attention to the mutuality (*Zweifuhlung*) of insightful perception and communications (*tele*) in the physician–patient as well as all other human relationships is one important approach to a necessary reappraisal of the general dynamics of interpersonal influence, of which "psychotherapy" is but a special instance.

Earl A. Loomis: [Moreno's example of transference and counter-transference in the therapist–patient relationship as that of two lovers] implies that there is *no basic difference* between the two partners in a therapeutic situation . . . it is still the therapist who assumes *responsibility for the helping* and the patient for the seeking and *receiving help*. There must always be mutuality and inter-dependence in an effective helping situation, but the fact that each partner has a *role* does not imply that there are no *differences* between the roles. [Moreno might have added that there is a tendency for] patients to *provoke* or *elicit* in their therapists (and in the general public) the sorts of reactions they need to recapitulate the past.

Mary L. Northway: *Tele* like the air is ever present . . . once having perceived it our facilities for studying it are not limited to the psychodrama or other specialized techniques, but move with us wherever we go, and can be investigated wherever we live socially.

W. Lynn Smith: *Group therapy research, because of its multiplicity of variables, needs a more global concept* [than transference], *such as "tele," from which logically valid sub-gestalts can be defined, observed, and measured.*

Walter Bromberg: Considering the therapeutic relationship wherein role playing is the primary data for study, we come to a more forthright view of doctor–patient relationship, more in harmony with our social living.

N. W. Ackerman: [The analysis of interpersonal relations must include current experience as well as the past] the actualities of behavior in the two-person therapeutic relationship are as significant in determining the outcome as the patterns of irrational unconscious motivation.

There are eight additional discussants for the first lecture, but this may be enough to give a flavor of their comments. Some are critical, most support the effort that Moreno is making to expand the list of concepts necessary for the analysis of group therapy. In his six pages of "replies," Moreno quotes excerpts from those who agree with him and notes some of the areas of disagreement, giving his response. For example, he asserts that he purposely overplayed the role of the patient in his analogy of two lovers. He ends his replies by reasserting that the way out of the confusion of terms is through carefully organized experimental research.

Lecture 2: Interpersonal therapy, group psychotherapy and the function of the unconscious

Moreno calls for a clarification of the constructs conscious, pre-conscious, and unconscious. However, his main interest is in interpersonal therapy and the possibilities of using psychodrama techniques to uncover the "co-unconscious." When a third person enters the therapeutic situation – for example, treating both a husband and wife where the relationship is highly structured and long standing – "interpersonal therapy" is required. This is a special category which might well be classified apart from individual and group psychotherapy. In this situation, the interpretation of resistance must move beyond the consideration of only the individual psyche, the individual unconscious, but we must assume that there is also a "deeper reality in which the unconsciouses of several individuals are interlocked, a 'co-unconscious.'" In his discussion of this concept, Moreno draws on the terminology of Freud, Jung, and Adler. Psychodrama techniques, including soliloquy, role reversal, double, and mirror, are described as a method of revealing the unconscious processes of each individual as well as the co-unconscious.

In the discussion included as a response to the second lecture, most of the 12 discussants use the occasion to continue their comments on the first lecture by adding second thoughts which repeat main responses to the first lecture. Some of the comments that deal specifically with the second lecture are given below.

Louis Cholden: What Moreno is dealing with is not the unconscious as a whole, but that aspect of the person which is hidden to himself but which is later available to conscious awareness, and that is essentially pointed at the living relationship with another person.

W. Lynn Smith: Moreno's quest for a more comprehensive understanding of both intra and inter-psychic phenomena is a relatively unexplored area. The appropriate unit for the study of the interactional process depends upon the problem being investigated. It may be the individual, the pair, or the group.

Robert James and W. Lynn Smith: The concept of a co-unconscious is brilliant. However Jung called attention to a similar phenomenon in the similarity that may occur between the unconscious of a parent and a child.

Wellman J. Warner: The task that Moreno has set, to reconcile ideas to achieve a single system of theory for psychotherapy is formidable. However it is necessary since psychotherapy deals with pathological states which are social in origin and require social treatment. All psychotherapy is group psychotherapy. An understanding of group dynamics is necessary for the doctor–patient dyad as it is for therapy in larger groups.

Moreno, in his five pages of replies, again quotes the discussants who favor his view. He uses the occasion to clarify some of the concepts that were not central to his lecture. For example, "role playing" does not mean that in a simulation the persons chosen for doctor and patient "play" at their roles. The patient really has a problem and the doctor really tries to help. The test of the validity of role playing is "existential." Existential validation claims validity *in situ*, in the here and now without any attempt to confirm the past or predict the future.

Lecture 3: The significance of the therapeutic format and the place of acting out in psychotherapy

The exposition in the third lecture takes the form of a bit of the history of Freud and psychoanalysis and a description of the main elements of psychodrama, with an example of how Moreno might have handled a problem Dr Breuer had with the acting out of Miss O. We have the impression that here and elsewhere in his writings, when Moreno felt that he was losing his audience he would give an account of an actual psychodrama, or in this case, one that he might have conducted, to recapture attention and to remind the audience that after all psychodrama is an action method and psychodramatic theory is best understood in action rather than in written words.

In his comments on Freud, Moreno notes that, in contrast to psychodrama which uses a stage, Freud used the couch which placed him in a superior position to the patient as the objective scientist who was outside the situation. Freud gave up hypnosis and used free association to avoid instances of acting out by his patients. However, Moreno suggests that there are some therapists and some patients best suited for the analytic type of work and others for a more histrionic approach. Psychodrama introduces auxiliary therapists who play the part of persons or objects that are significant for the protagonist. The protagonist is encouraged to express real feelings toward these auxiliaries, thus lessening the possibility of transference toward the director of the psychodrama. By acting out dreams and feelings in a controlled situation, the material becomes more accessible for analysis and the patient is less likely to act out in an everyday context.

In his introduction to the discussion of the third lecture, Moreno refers to a group session of eight psychiatrists, psychologists, and sociologists, including himself, as if they were physically present at the same discussion; however, some of their contributions are quite formal, including bibliographies, suggesting that they are responding to Moreno's written lectures. In any case, several of them continue to discuss the relationship between *tele* and transference, although the main focus in the third lecture was on acting out. It would appear that some of the discussants received the texts of all of the lectures at one time and based most of their comments on the first lecture. Here we had planned to record only the comments that refer to the third lecture. Unfortunately, none of the seven discussants whose comments are included in Moreno's volume have anything to say about acting out.

Moreno nevertheless provides "replies," noting especially the comments that approve of his approach. In response to some comments comparing his ideas to those of Adler, he reminds us that he was not a follower of Freud, nor anyone else. "I was forced to create a place of my own in the world of psychotherapy and social science, or perish. He who is not a son has to become a father himself. That is why I became a father very early."

Lectures 4, 5, and 6
The fourth "lecture" is an article describing the use of role reversal by Zerka and JL in raising their son Jonathan to be a "spontaneous man," with comments by social scientists, P. A. Sorokin, Read Bain, Jiri Nehnevajsa, and Robert R. Blake.

The fifth "lecture" is an account of a psychodrama with a man who thought he was Adolf Hitler, reprinted from *Progress in Psychotherapy* (Fromm-Reichmann and Moreno, 1956), with a comment by Jiri Nehnevajsa.

The sixth "lecture" deals with "Existentialism, daseinsalyse and psychodrama," with discussions by Medard Boss, Jiri Nehnevajsa, and Jiri Kolaja. For Moreno, psychodrama provides a bridge between the existentialists' emphasis on subjective understanding of existence at the moment and the empirical scientists who require some objective criteria. Since every session of psychodrama is a unique experience for the participants, further validation of individual and group psychotherapeutic practice is not imperative, as long as no generalizations are made or predictions made for the future. If the therapeutic experiences are valid for the participants and they take its value as self-evident (existential validation), then a scientific validation would be meaningless for the participants. However, scientific validation and existential validation do not exclude one another, but can be construed as a continuum.

Moreno adds a summary to the volume in which he contrasts psychodrama with psychoanalysis. He asserts that the fundamental principle underlying all methods of psychotherapy is not transference but encounter involving *tele*.

Criticisms of Moreno's style of writing

When asked why the first edition of *Who Shall Survive?* (1934) was so clumsily written, Moreno gave a teasing reply that he had left his fingerprint on every page so that there would be no question that it had been written by him alone. Nevertheless, he recalled, "there have been, to my knowledge, at least three individuals who claimed that they had written the book" (Moreno, 1953: lxxxvii). Although he acknowledged Helen Jennings as his collaborator, in his presentation of the evidence Moreno neglected to point out that there was another set of fingerprints on the 1934 edition in the form of three appendices written by Helen Jennings. The first of these, "A survey of children groups", is included without citation in the 1953 edition (1953: 175–202).

To fully understand Moreno's writing, one must use his own method of role reversal. Then to interpret his writings to others one can facilitate Moreno's self-presentation by doubling, verbalizing his thoughts about the materials he is presenting and providing the connections between parts of the work that would otherwise appear to be disconnected. We say "one" (not "you," not "we") in the spirit of anonymity that Moreno advocated. Anonymity in the sense that it can be and should be the action of everyone. Ideally, in Moreno's vision, everyone should be able to be the facilitator for everyone else, so that all people can be spontaneous and realize their creative potential.

There is a sense in which no ordinary writing can capture the spirit of the sociometric/psychodramatic enterprise. Moreno believed that the only reality was that of the experience of the moment, the experience of being a co-creator of a social reality. Psychodrama is a method of re-creation, allowing, it is hoped, for more spontaneity and creativity than during the first time around, on the grounds that "every second time is a liberation from the first." Thus the only way to fully understand psychodrama is to experience it and the only way to fully understand a community based on sociometric principles is to help create one. However, we cannot all be "there and then" so sometimes we try to convey the experience by using words in the "here and now."

Of the styles of writing, scientific argument is the most formal, the most bound by cultural conserves, and therefore the least likely to capture the spirit of the moment. A literary form of a story, packed with metaphor and analogy, comes closer. Much of Moreno's writing is in this form. However, poetry comes closest since the subject is sketched with broad strokes of the brush, with contrasting colors. The connections between ideas are often implicit rather than explicit, and depend upon the reader's cultural heritage and present empathy, insight, and intuition to provide the linkages.

Readers of Moreno's writing who did not expect to be called upon to double him were put off by his style that reflected more spontaneity than reasoned argument. Shaffer and Galinsky (1974: 111) observe: "although he has written voluminously, he has not written with the greatest clarity and directness of expression."

Meyer (1952: 359), in a comment on Moreno's discussion of the social atom of death, as reprinted in *Sociometry, Experimental Method and the Science of Society* (1951b), observes that "unfortunately, this and other equally provocative applications of sociometric theory to the analysis of social relationships appear as fragments." Of the whole collection of articles by Moreno, Meyer records: "this book will disappoint those who look to it for the long-needed systematic statement of approach, theory and methodology which Dr Moreno calls sociometry" (1952: 355). In a footnote, Meyer tells us that such a statement was promised in the revised edition of *Who Shall Survive?* (1953), then in press. Unfortunately, Moreno never wrote an organized book. All of his "books", with the exception of the first edition of *Who Shall Survive?* (1934) based on research conducted with Helen Jennings, are mainly collections of reprints of articles.

After *Who Shall Survive?* (1953) was published, Warner reviewed it for the *British Journal of Sociology* (1954). He noted that the first edition in 1934 was an important book and that the expanded version was still an important book. He then warned the reader:

> First, let it be clear that *Who Shall Survive?* does not fit any of the notions of what constitutes the conventional study in a well-regulated discipline. It is not a systematic treatise threading its way from proposition to exposition with logical parsimony. It is a highly personal document. It brings together a collection of writings, spaced over half a life-time, variously descriptive, narrative and commentative, editorially linked together in the form of an apologia, declaration of faith, polemic, case history, practitioner's observations, and theoretical formulation – all encased in an autobiographical unity of advocacy and controversy. It will be the despair of the limited specialist with his horror of untidy academic housekeeping. (Warner, 1954: 228)

However, there is more to the story, as Warner recalled in a presentation entitled "J. L. Moreno – the universal man" made on the occasion of a memorial service for Moreno in 1974 (Warner, personal communication, 25 June 1978).

> Let me recount an amusing but revealing incident. Twenty years ago Morris Ginsberg, the dean of British sociology, wrote me from London to ask that I give him a review of the then newly issued *Who Shall Survive?* for the *British Journal of Sociology*. When I first sat down to write it, the typewriter ran away with me – it must have added up to nearly 20 pages. I sent it to Ginsberg with the notation that I would understand if it was too long for publication. Back came a letter from Morris saying he wanted to publish it, not as a review but as the lead article for the next issue. "But," pleaded Morris, "just one thing. Please let me omit the last paragraph." Reluctantly I agreed. But then I took the whole piece to JL. He read it in complete absorption until he came to the last paragraph. Then he began to chortle with that unrestrained merriment and laughter which was characteristic of him, and clapped his hands in glee. When I said, "But Ginsberg wants to omit that last paragraph," he exclaimed, "But why? That's just right." I pulled that article in offprint from my file the other day, along with my original manuscript. I want to read that expurgated final paragraph, because it points up the one thing I want to say today.
> Here it is: "At once a hazard and a fascination to the reader is the image of the man which emerges out of this book – an essentially autobiographical document. The roles he plays run a range of inconsistencies and incongruities taken separately – and a highly ingrate image when perceived as a man. To the methodological investigator of the laboratory there is added the wide-ranging intuitions of the poet; to the detached experimenter is added the devotional commitment of religious faith; to the self-forgetting prober for facts there is contrasted the overly sensitive claimant for credit; to the generosity of acknowledging debts to others is added a violent resentment towards others who have not acknowledged him; and to his matter of fact assumption of the eminence

of genius is added a humility that manifests itself in humor ranging from sly digs at his own pomposity, from allusions of messianism to laughter at his own pretentiousness. It is no wonder that he has inspired so much attachment from his disciples and so bitter dislike from those who know him least."

5

The Overall Influence of J. L. Moreno

Some 60 years have passed since Moreno introduced sociometry as a method of measuring interpersonal relationships in small groups, organizations, and communities, and psychodrama as a form of group therapy. The people who were trained by Moreno as psychodrama directors have trained others. The fifth generation of psychodrama directors is being trained. Psychodrama spread from the United States to Canada, Europe, South America, Australia, Israel, and other areas. It is estimated that the number of professional practitioners who use psychodrama in some form is between 5,000 and 10,000.

Sociometry, in contrast, had its heyday in the 1940s and 1950s. References to the study of interpersonal choice under the heading "sociometry" have all but disappeared from the current social psychological literature, although the subject matter continues to be of interest under the heading "intimate relations." Sociodrama was never developed fully by Moreno or by his followers. A form of drama that bears some relationship to sociodrama and to Impromptu Theater, "Playback Theater," instituted by Jonathan Fox, a student of Zerka Moreno, has become popular. In Playback Theater, a team of actors, auxiliaries in Moreno's terms, act on a stage the thoughts, feelings, or incidents suggested by members of the audience (Salas, 1993; Fox, 1995).

As a context for judging the overall influence of J. L. Moreno, note that psychodrama is a performing art. Thus, in common with other performing arts, including music, dance, and "happenings," the main effect is on the actors and the audience at the time. Do they obtain catharsis and insight? Does their involvement in the performance change their relationships with each other? For evidence we would need the accounts of the experience from actors and audience. In the case of psychodrama, we are especially interested in the protagonist, the auxiliaries, and the director. Unfortunately, we have very few documents of this kind. In addition, people like Moreno who are at their best in a spontaneous encounter of the moment, are not equally adept at setting out formal statements of theory or method. Since Moreno provided no shortage of written material, most of the judgments of his work are based on his own writings and not on observations and evaluations of the man in action. However, unlike a virtuoso performer in music, art, dance, or theater, our evaluation must include an assessment not only of his "work" at the time of performance, but also of the extent to which he established a "school," a line of thought and action that could be carried on by others.

Sociometry is also an action method as used by Moreno. Although some paper and pencil work might be involved in gathering data for a "sociogram," Moreno stressed that the choices should be made with regard to some criterion on which action should be based. If the group, organization, or society was not going to be restructured on the basis of the sociometric data, Moreno asserted that this was not true sociometry. So, once again, we need evidence of the effect of sociometric reorganization on individuals and groups. Instead, much of the literature deals with the standard questions of reliability and validity of the instrument rather than on the effect of using it. Further, many of the studies labeled "sociometric" were only "near sociometric" in Moreno's view since they simply asked people to choose others they "liked" rather than specifying a criterion. Sociometry was certainly effective in helping school teachers, social workers, and military personnel officers visualize the social networks in the groups they worked with. But the method appeared to be so simple that many people used it and many studies were published without providing an adequate description of the method or its effectiveness. As a result, secondary analysis of the material becomes difficult.

We will begin this chapter with an indication of the contemporary use of sociometry, psychodrama, and Moreno's contribution to the development of group psychotherapy in whatever form it was used. Next we document Moreno's contribution to social psychology and group psychotherapy through sociometry and the emphasis on the importance of roles by citing two reviews of his work written in the 1950s, and by indicating current applications of sociometry. We will close the chapter with excerpts from three articles written *in memoriam*, an "epilogue" written on the occasion of Moreno's death, and some remarks at a memorial service.

The impact of Moreno's sociometry

After Moreno introduced the Sociometric Test, the method became so popular that his work was followed by some thousands of articles using some version of a sociometric or "near sociometric" test, primarily during the years 1950 through 1970. Reviews of the methods and substantive findings are given in the following selections: Glanzer and Glazer (1959), Moreno et al. (1960), Bjerstedt (1963), Borgatta (1968), Lindzey and Byrne (1968), Bramel (1969), Byrne and Griffitt (1973), Hare (1976), Hale (1985) and Hare et al. (1994).

In the 1970s and 1980s, the interest in friendship groups and the underlying currents of attraction in formal organizations continued, but the studies were no longer labeled as "sociometric." The research, carried out primarily on university campuses with men and women who were dating, engaged to be married, or married, centers on the process of forming intimate bonds. The area of study was now labeled "close relationships" (Levinger, 1980; Kelley et al., 1983). A close relationship is one in which the two persons are willing to engage in self-disclosure. The function of friendship groups is now studied under the heading "support groups."

However, in the late 1980s there was an attempt to revive interest in sociometry through articles published in the *Journal of Group Psychotherapy, Psychodrama and Sociometry*. Hart (1987) edited a special issue of the journal on sociometry, indicating current applications of sociometry in career development, group topology, and the use of computer programs for the analysis of sociometric data. In another issue of the journal, Mendelson (1989) called for an application of the "sociometric vision" of sociometry as an action science in the workplace. He urged the sociometrist as analyst and therapist to facilitate change among groups in industry. Blake and McCanse (1989) recorded a number of possibilities for "the rediscovery of sociometry," especially as it might be used by management and human resource professionals.

Remer (1995) called for the use of "strong" rather than "weak" sociometry. In the "strong" version, choices should be acted upon, rather than simply collected to show preferences. Remer maintained that the value of the strong version is not so much in producing effective groups as in the "warm up" of the individuals to make choices which reflect the amount of *tele* present. He suggests applications to promote self-knowledge and intrapersonal and intrapsychic insight.

Readers of the current literature will find that Moreno had already begun to investigate most of the important aspects of friendship in his work at the Hudson School. For example, there is still a need to distinguish an acquaintance from a friend, as Moreno did with the Acquaintance Test, to understand the underlying motivations for choice, as Moreno did in his motivation analysis, and to plot on a graph the degree of involvement over time, as

Moreno did in his diagrams representing the interaction pattern of two individuals.

Moreno stated clearly that any test, including his own sociometric tests, only revealed the end product of interaction and not the interaction itself. He was more interested in the process. As one way of revealing what actually went on in relationships between one person and a set of others, he devised the "Spontaneity Test." In a less complicated format, this procedure is found in current research in role plays and laboratory experiments in which subjects with different degrees of intimate relationship are observed while they discuss revealing material or carry out other joint tasks.

Moreno did more than design a number of interesting tests. Recall that his goal at Hudson was the sociometric reconstruction of the community. By the time a new girl had made her way through the variety of situational tests, from the Entrance Test to the Exit Test, she had presumably become quite familiar with role playing and the fact that Moreno was trying to make her stay at Hudson as productive as possible. She must have received the message that she was important and her social atom was important. She had learned how to adjust her behavior in interaction with different persons in different situations. She was learning the social skills that she had presumably lacked when she was sent to the school for "training."

Anyone currently working in the social or psychological services at a residential school, psychiatric hospital, prison, or any other type of closed community, would do well to re-read Moreno's work, not only to find suggestions for tests of social relationships that might be adapted to some current situation, but also to absorb his overall approach to the enhancement of individual creativity through the social construction of reality in the community.

Psychodrama and group therapy

Many of Moreno's ideas and techniques found their way into the "human potential movement" and various "action" therapies. For example, the founder of the modern Gestalt therapy approach, Fritz Perls, used the "empty chair" as one of his principal techniques. Eric Berne (1970: 164) noted that Perls shared with other "active" psychotherapists the "Moreno problem: the fact that nearly all known 'active' techniques were first tried out by Moreno in psycho-drama, so that it is difficult to come up with an original idea in this regard." Abraham Maslow (1968), a leading figure in humanistic psychology, makes a similar point: "I would like to add one credit-where-credit-is-due footnote. Many of the techniques . . . were originally invented by Dr Jacob Moreno. . . ." Will Schutz (1971: 108), a leader in the encounter movement, wrote that "virtually all of the methods that I had proudly compiled or invented [Moreno] had more or less anticipated, in some cases forty years earlier. . . ."

Moreno's contribution to group psychotherapy through promoting a group therapy organization and group therapy conferences has been recorded in Chapter 1 as part of the history of his life. His contribution through the invention of psychodrama has been indicated in Chapter 3 as a major contribution to practice. Additional evidence of the contribution of psychodrama can be found in issues of the *Journal of Group Psychotherapy, Psychodrama and Sociometry* edited by Guldner on uses of psychodramatic techniques in university education (1990a) and with adolescents (1990b).

Many texts and collections of articles about group psychotherapy contain a chapter on psychodrama. Some of these chapters were written by Moreno during his lifetime (see for example, Moreno, 1955a, 1957a, 1959b, 1967) and later some by Zerka Moreno (see Moreno, 1978, 1983). Moreno also edited collections of articles and handbooks dealing with group psychotherapy (see Moreno, 1945a; Fromm-Reichmann and Moreno, 1956; Masserman and Moreno, 1957–60; Moreno et al., 1966). Fox (1987) provides a collection of Moreno's writing under the title *The Essential Moreno*, and Ann Hale, based on conversations with Moreno, condensed the 1953 edition of *Who Shall Survive?* from 763 pages to 325 as a "student edition" (Moreno, 1993).

Moreno's students, and their students in turn, have written their own accounts of psychodrama, sociodrama, or sociometry, often combining the approach with their own theory of social interaction, or with concepts drawn from another therapeutic approach, or with a focus on some special population (see Kahn, 1964; Blatner, 1973; Greenberg, 1974; Haskell, 1975; Yablonsky, 1976; Leveton, 1977; Starr, 1977; Rabson, 1979; Goldman and Morrison, 1984; Hale, 1985; Kipper, 1986; Blatner and Blatner, 1988; Sternberg and Garcia, 1989; Williams, 1989; Fuhlrodt, 1990; Holmes and Karp, 1991; Kellermann, 1992; Holmes et al., 1994).

Shaffer and Galinsky, in their introduction to their text on *Models of Group Therapy and Sensitivity Training* (1974), noted that "psychodrama, in a strict historical sense is the oldest model extant" (1974: 7).

> The influence of psychodrama as a whole has been diffuse, and certainly less pronounced than that of the psychoanalytic and experiential models. The method's greatest impact has been on the creation of a special technique, usually referred to as "role-playing", that is frequently employed by group leaders in conjunction with a variety of other procedures. (1974: 8)

The most significant emphases introduced by Moreno were on action, empathic identification, and catharsis. Through empathic identification with the protagonist, the audience members gain help, and through their assumption of auxiliary ego roles also give help to the protagonist.

Comparing psychodrama's focus on the protagonist with other forms of group psychotherapy, Shaffer and Galinsky suggested that psychodrama was not unique since "almost all models of group interaction . . . involve a scenario in which one particular member, for however brief a period, assumes 'stage center' while the remainder of the group focuses on him" (1974: 8). Not every one has agreed. Walton, in his collection of articles on *Small Group Psychotherapy*, records that "patients have been helped to act out their life problems and personal conflicts with others on a stage . . . such 'psychodrama' is not group therapy" (1971: 17). However, for practitioners of psychodrama, the value of psychodrama as a form of group therapy is not questioned. Blatner's conclusion to his overview of psychodrama is typical (Blatner and Blatner, 1988: 9):

> In summary, the process of psychodrama is enormously complex because of the many facets of life that it can address and manipulate. On the other hand, its essence is relatively simple: Help the patient experience his or her situation as vividly as possible; help unspoken thoughts be expressed; help group members to help each other; help patients to develop and apply their own creativity to their life challenges. Psychodrama is a broad group of methodologies that facilitates the principles of dynamic psychotherapy.

After Moreno's death, the organization of psychodramatists became more democratic with a more decentralized distribution of authority (Blatner and Blatner, 1988: 27). The American Society for Group Psychotherapy in Psychodrama (ASGPP), the organization that Moreno had founded in 1942, became more professional in its orientation. The American Board of Examiners in Psychodrama, Sociometry, and Group Psychotherapy was established in 1975 as an organization to test and certify practitioners and trainers. In 1976, the Federation of Trainers and Training Programs in Psychodrama (FTTPP) was established to standardize curricula in the various training institutes.

Social psychology

One comparison of the theories of Moreno and George Herbert Mead that was published in 1941, and two reviews of Moreno's work that appeared in the 1950s, give an indication of the way in which his contribution was viewed by his contemporaries. In the comparison of Moreno and Mead, Leonard Cottrell and Ruth Goodenough (1941), both social psychologists, suggest that Moreno's contribution was to provide a method for the analysis of the social act that formed the basis of Mead's theory. The two review articles were written by professors of sociology at New York University at the time that Moreno was teaching in the graduate program. Henry Meyer (1952), writing about "the sociometries of Dr Moreno," as a review of *Sociometry, Experimental Method and the Science of Society* (Moreno, 1951b), reminds us that sociometry must be understood on at least three interrelated levels: as an orientation toward life, as a theory of society, and as a method of research. Wellman Warner (1954), writing about the relationship between "sociology and psychiatry" in a review of Moreno's work occasioned by the publication of the second edition of *Who Shall Survive?* (1953), shows how Moreno's theory gives insight into the way an individual as a person in a role combines social perception with a commitment to act to create new interpersonal realities.

Mead's theory and Moreno's method
Cottrell and Goodenough (1941) considered the social psychology of George Herbert Mead (1950) to be the most comprehensive and valuable theory that had yet appeared in the field. Moreno's method of psychodrama allowed him to explore concretely the dimensions of a behavioral role. For the protagonist in the psychodrama, the opportunity to act out whole units of behavior, which in other forms of therapy receive only partial or symbolic fulfillment, has a distinct cathartic effect. Further, the use of auxiliary egos almost does away with the analyst's function as an observer. There is a mutual participation in the dramatic episodes which anyone, including the patient, may attempt to elucidate. Moreno's work gains significance because he has hit upon an experimental technique that can be used with the same descriptive unit that Mead himself used in a much broader social psychological theory. Moreno made concrete the social act and the social situation that provides the context for interaction. Thus the conclusions of both men can be amended or enlarged in the light of the contributions of each. In particular, Meadian theory can be amended to take into account the pathology as well as the promise of the role-taking process.

The sociometries of Moreno
Meyer (1952) describes Moreno's 1951 collection of 31 articles, papers, and speeches as "part of Dr Moreno's continuing 'war of persuasion' to convince everyone of the basic validity of sociometry

and the imperative necessity for its application to benefit mankind" (Meyer, 1952: 354). Although the 1951 book might disappoint those who looked for a systematic statement of the approach, theory, and methodology of sociometry, it does serve as a reminder that sociometry is more than a set of special research techniques. Sociometry combines an orientation toward life, a theory of society, and a method of research, which for Moreno are completely integrated in his own holistic viewpoint.

For Meyer, the first sociometry is a philosophy of living. This version of sociometry springs from a belief in the spontaneous and creative forces in human beings and the desire to release these forces from the confines of institutions and culture. A key idea is spontaneity which is never made entirely explicit, although it is revealed by vitality of action in a situation. Sociometry was intended to deal with two basic maladjustments in the society of Moreno's time: the destructiveness of technology, and the loss of God in human theology. After identifying the patterns of social structure that exist in human society, natural spontaneity could be released, to make it possible to reorganize human relationships and institutions in accordance with the highest human ideals.

This social reconstruction is dependent upon the involvement of all people. However, Moreno was not manipulative, his social researcher, an "action agent," is a co-actor, co-subject, and co-scientist with all others in the sociometric experiment. Sensitivity to the needs of all is the result of a "warming up" process.

The second sociometry of Moreno, according to Meyer, is a theory of society. On the basis of *tele*, attractions and repulsions between persons, social atoms and psychological networks emerge that are the structure of human society. This primary level of society is revealed through sociometric, action-based procedures. The sociometric structures are as real as the secondary structures, the "external society," the more formal groupings and institutional patterns, built upon them. The "dynamic synthesis and interpretation" of these levels is "the social reality." Differences between the sociometric level and the external society can lead to maladjustment. Moreno's hypothesis is that "social conflict and tension increases in direct proportion to the sociodynamic difference between official society and sociometric matrix" (Meyer, 1952: 359). The resolution of the differences is not a static balance because both the spontaneous and creative forces in human interaction are a continuous source of new sociometric relationships.

The third sociometry is a method of research. However, Meyer notes that although sociograms, action and role-playing tests, and other techniques are widely used in research, the ingenuity of the techniques is often mistaken for the substance of the sociometric method. The heart of the sociometric method is action where the researcher becomes a participant to combine research, diagnosis, therapeutic and political procedures into a single process. Moreno was aware that this conception of sociometry ran counter to the conventional ideas about scientific method which separate the researcher from the subject.

At the end of his review, Meyer calls for a clearer systematic statement of the theory of sociometry, with definitions of the special terms introduced, and more exposition of the fundamental concepts, such as *tele*, spontaneity, and action research.

Sociology and psychiatry

Warner (1954) begins his review of the revised edition of *Who Shall Survive?* (1953) with the observation that Moreno is not so much concerned with the analysis of behavior into parts, but how the parts can be put together in action. The basis of behavior is religious. The individual is one unit in the process of interaction; the group is a set of interactions. Sociology thus is defined as the study of the unities and processes of interpersonal relations. Psychiatry, in this context, becomes a branch of sociology that deals with the application of this knowledge to the solution of problems of individuals or groups with their interpersonal relations.

In Moreno's theory, there are four crucial aspects of action: (a) the *actors* as individuals in roles; (b) the *commitment* of the actors as they warm up to a definition of the situation; (c) the *acting out* as the actors enact fully what they bring to and find in the situation (Moreno's "reality principle"); and (d) the *moment*, since the action cannot be viewed from either the past or the future, it is "*in statu nascendi.*"

Moreno's idea of spontaneity is that of a concept of organization. It is the way in which the actor participates in a "reality" that meets the needs of both the personality and the group. Creativity is the quality of action that produces new realities.

The act is not merely an outcome, but a series of stages. The analysis of the act must include the readiness of each individual – his or her perception, motivation, and goal – to be involved in the interaction. This state of readiness may change from moment to moment, depending on the extent to which the actor has reciprocal empathy, *tele*, with the other actors that form the most elementary social unit, the social atom.

Warner continues his review with a description of the techniques introduced by Moreno for the analysis of social data and intervention for the purpose of therapy, efficiency, play, or learning. The Sociometric Test reveals the network of interpersonal attractions and repulsions, an indication of the individual's readiness to engage in interaction. Psychodrama, focusing on the individual, and sociodrama, focusing on the group, make it possible to replicate the interaction for the analysis of successive stages and to introduce controls, either for study or treatment purposes. Group psychotherapy, of which psychodrama is one form, is designed, in Moreno's words, for "protecting and simulating the self-regulating mechanisms of natural groups – through the use of one man as a therapeutic agent of the other, of the group as the therapeutic agent of the other" (Warner, 1954: 235). The participant researchers themselves are the only adequate instruments of discrimination and measurement. Psychodrama and role playing can also be used for the analysis of the researcher.

In his summary appraisal, Warner declares that a range of interests and ideas are revealed in a reading of *Who Shall Survive?* and that "in its breathless drive, the work of the clinician, the practitioner, the evangelist and the scientific investigator are not neatly set apart" (Warner, 1954: 236). Warner notes that appraisal properly begins by discriminating between clinical usefulness and theoretical adequacy. Moreno's insights had proved their clinical usefulness in the practice of group psychotherapy as evidenced by the review of Dreikurs and Corsini (1954) of 20 years of group psychotherapy. On the side of theoretical adequacy, a major contribution of Moreno was to:

> make explicit and cogent the proposition that in dealing with this kind of data there is a natural alliance between the therapist and the investigator, so that the scientific enterprise is one in which the clinical and therapeutical interest is a necessary component of the procedures of scientific investigation. (Warner, 1954: 237).

During the early period, Moreno's methods were very much in vogue. Psychodrama was widely used in veterans' hospitals in the United Sates as a method of psychiatric treatment during and after the Second World War. Sociodrama was used in schools, universities, and community groups to act out incidents in race relations or other social problem areas to provide case material for analysis. The Sociometric Test was also frequently used in the American school system to form reading groups and by the American army to select men as replacements for military units.

As noted at the beginning of this chapter, the contributions that Moreno made in developing psychodrama and promoting group therapy are still very much in evidence, with most psychodramatists still using the basic techniques developed by Moreno with few alterations. Moreno's publications on psychodrama were often cited in the social science literature. For the period from 1973, when the *Social Science Citation Index* was first published, until 1983, about half of the citations of Moreno's work were to his books and articles on psychodrama. Most of the other citations were to the first or second edition of *Who Shall Survive?* and the remainder to works on sociometry.

In memoriam

We close this chapter with excerpts from three articles written *in memoriam*, from an "epilogue" written after Moreno's death, and from some words delivered at a memorial service. In introducing the three articles by Borgatta et al. (1975), the editor of the journal *Sociometry* noted that "the three statements . . . vary in their emphasis, but all carry a picture of a man who attempted to exemplify his own first principle: our basic nature is fulfilled only through our ability to be creative and spontaneous" (Borgatta et al., 1975: 148).

Three contributions of Jacob L. Moreno

Borgatta (Borgatta et al., 1975) identifies the first contribution of Moreno as his influence in the development of theories of behavior, as an alternative to the then prevailing views of Freud, especially as they relate to the therapeutically oriented professions. The second contribution is another way of phrasing the first. He developed his own approaches through a succession of experiences that led to "accidental" discoveries. As well as being experimental, he was observant. Although he emphasized spontaneity and creativity, he seemed always aware of patterns and designs. He was able to recognize the efficacy of theatrical techniques for therapeutic ends. His technique of role playing is used for many purposes and in many circumstances – an enormous contribution.

Moreno was sensitive to the forces of social control that are part of the social order. In the use of psychodrama and sociodrama, he demonstrated his knowledge, sometimes intuitive and sometimes derived from more systematic observation, of behavior in groups. Not only may the group be used as a source of social support, legitimation, and sanction but also the group setting may be used to allow the individual to have insight, to learn, and to practice behavior.

The third contribution is the development of the sociometric approach. Here the development is not of a single procedure, but of a whole class of procedures. Moreno's major impact on academic research rests on this work. The sociometric approach makes it possible for psychotherapeutic applications to be more realistically grounded in the empirical world. His point of beginning was the social atom. These atoms joined at various levels to become the fabric of the social order.

Among Moreno's many contributions, the fundamental importance of two is beyond debate. "Samuel A. Stouffer once commented to a somewhat overwhelmed young student regarding Moreno: Whatever else, how many of us can look forward to leaving two such important contributions as role-playing and the Sociometric Test?" (Borgatta et al., 1975: 151–2).

Moreno, sociometric methodology, and the redesign of society

Boguslaw (Borgatta et al., 1975) observes that, although social scientists could develop a scientific discipline dedicated to the measurement and analysis of verbal choices of others in interpersonal situations, which seemed to be the preoccupation of articles in the then current issues of *Sociometry*, this was clearly not what Moreno had in mind when he started it all. To understand Moreno's conception of sociometry, one must understand his self-image as a healer and philosopher. The validity of sociometric tests or of action techniques depended on their usefulness in restructuring society. In a society in which human beings did not change, but became completely predictable, losing their spontaneity and creativity, individuals would become somewhat less than human. Rather than observe society "objectively," Moreno chose to actively take social destiny in his own hands, to initiate experiments, and simultaneously check their validity. Boguslaw observes that "evoking a vision of Moreno *passively* waiting for anything, becomes an exercise in short-cutting the imagination" (Borgatta et al., 1975: 154).

Moreno chose to live in America where the central ethos revolved around industrial production and its concomitant rationalization of everyday life. Thus his most profound contributions that might help people throw off "the shackles of psychological bondage – the cultural conserves" (Borgatta et al., 1975: 155) were always destined for marginality.

> Thus the greatness and tragedy of Moreno was that he chose to work as a non-marginal man in a society in which he was destined for marginality. He lived to see the less important aspects of his work enshrined in the hearts of academic, business and government establishments, while his most significant efforts still remain part of that marginality to which their very creativity condemns them. (Borgatta et al., 1975: 156)

Moreno's image of humanity

For Haskell (Borgatta et al., 1975), Moreno must be considered as one of the greatest intellectual innovators of the twentieth century. Although his work appeared to some as broken into many pieces which did not mesh, there was one unifying theme, his image of humanity. Moreno advocated a new religion modified by the insights of science. The creative portion in each person was God representing the infinite capacity for creativity. Everyone is continuously participating in the creation of the world of the future. In the ideal sociometric society, all people would be given the opportunity to participate to the best of their abilities; all should survive. Aided by sociometric analysis of the relationship between individuals and their social atoms, and social atoms and the network of society, he sought to combine in one society high individual freedom with high cohesion.

Group psychotherapy, psychodrama, sociodrama, and other inventions were developed to provide people with opportunities to explore social relationships in a laboratory setting. They provided an opportunity for healing produced by forces of the group itself. Moreno's system "was designed to treat not only the disturbed individual nor even the poorly functioning group but actually all of mankind" (Borgatta et al., 1975: 160).

An epilogue

Writing an "epilogue" for his book on *Psychodrama* (1976: 274–85), Yablonsky recalls that, as a graduate student, he had first met Moreno in 1949 when he enrolled in Moreno's seminar of psychodrama at New York University. Yablonsky trained with Moreno at Beacon and "joined the psychodrama movement with great enthusiasm." "The thing I remember most about Moreno . . . were his eyes. I never met anyone who looked at me so directly, honestly, and with such intensity" (Yablonsky, 1976: 279). Yablonsky goes on to say that Moreno was a highly significant role model, whether lecturing to students, working with patients, writing books; all of these activities were integrated with a religious zeal. In the 1950s, many therapists were threatened by and hostile toward Moreno who was recommending a group approach when the prevailing forms of therapy were individually oriented. However, in the brief span of 20 years, many therapists came to recognize the validity and significance of group process and psychodrama and the use of these concepts and methods as adjuncts to their practice.

The last time that Yablonsky saw Moreno was in April 1974. Moreno was 85 years old. A series of minor strokes had confined him to bed. The American Society of Group Psychotherapy and Psychodrama, which Moreno had founded, was meeting in New York. Hundreds of former students, friends, and professional associates filed through his bedroom one by one to pay their respects. When Yablonsky arrived, Moreno told him that this was no time for sadness: "I have lived a full life. I've done my job. It's time for me to go on to something else" (Yablonsky, 1976: 284). Yablonsky spent the afternoon reading Moreno's as yet unpublished biography in which Moreno has a vision that he has died and gone to heaven. There, even Freud acknowledges that "If I had lived longer, I too would have most certainly become a psychodramatist like Moreno" (Yablonsky, 1976: 285).

J. L. Moreno – the universal man

Wellman J. Warner was asked to speak at a memorial service organized by Zerka in the grounds of the Institute at Beacon two months after Moreno's death.

> It was a psychodramatic encounter. In a large tent crowded with people from everywhere who had known Moreno, Zerka had placed a chair in the front – an empty chair, with Zerka on one side and Warner on the other. One by one, a long succession of people came forward, usually reaching out to touch the occupant of the empty chair – and speak to him, thanking him for what he had done to their lives, recalling events and creating an atmosphere of celebration without lamentation. It was a memorial service which was in fact memorable. (Warner, personal communication, 25 June 1978)

In his address, Warner described the meeting as a "moment" of generating commitment. Many labels had been attached to Moreno because in his life's work he could not be fitted neatly into the mold of any one specialized field. "The really distinguishing fact is that he broke all the conventional stereotypes in order to live and deal with the universal in man – the ordinary man in all places and states" (Warner, personal communication, 25 June 1978). He was a "great soul with all his human emotions," who could see and enjoy his own frailties because he was so completely identified with all men. For Moreno, life and creativity is in the reality of the subjective. Every one of his major concepts is a symbolic representation of that only final reality – subjectivity. "Man's experience of himself, of reality, of God, of the universe – is subjective, in the here and now ... Moreno is that extraordinary voice – the ordinary man speaking in the role of the universal man" (Warner, personal communication, 25 June 1978).

Select Bibliography of J. L. Moreno

This bibliography is a short list of Moreno's major work. The complete bibliograpy of Moreno's work is provided in Hare (1986a). Copies of published and unpublished material of Moreno's are collected in the Francis A. Countway Library of Medicine, Harvard Medical School, Boston.

Moreno, J. L. (1934) *Who Shall Survive? A New Approach to the Problem of Human Interrelations*. Washington, DC: Nervous and Mental Disease Publishing Co.

Moreno, J. L. (ed.) (1945) *Group Psychotherapy: a Symposium*. Beacon, NY: Beacon House.

Moreno, J. L. (1947) *The Theatre of Spontaneity*. Beacon, NY: Beacon House. (Reprinted as third edition in 1980.)

Moreno, J. L. (1951) *Sociometry, Experimental Method and the Science of Society*. Beacon, NY: Beacon House.

Moreno, J. L. (1953) *Who Shall Survive? Foundations of Sociometry, Group Psychotherapy, and Sociodrama*. Beacon, NY: Beacon House. (Revised from 1934 edition. Reprinted as third edition in 1978.)

Moreno, J. L. (1956) *Sociometry and the Science of Man*. Beacon, NY: Beacon House.

Moreno, J. L. (1957) *The First Book on Group Psychotherapy: 1932*. Beacon, NY: Beacon House.

Moreno, J. L. (1964) "The third psychiatric revolution and the scope of psychodrama", *Group Psychotherapy*, 17(2–3): 149–71.

Moreno, J. L. (1970) "The triadic system, psychodrama–sociometry–group psychotherapy", *Group Psychotherapy and Psychodrama*, 23(1–2): 16.

Moreno, J. L. (1971) *The Words of the Father*. Beacon, NY: Beacon House. (First published 1941.)

Moreno, J. L. (1972) *Psychodrama: First Volume*. Beacon, NY: Beacon House. (First edition 1946.)

Moreno, J. L. (1989) "The autobiography of J. L. Moreno, MD" (edited by J. D. Moreno), *Journal of Group Psychotherapy, Psychodrama and Sociometry*, 42(1): 3–52 and 42(2): 59–126.

Moreno, J. L. (1993) *Who Shall Survive?* (student edition, edited by Ann Hale). McLean, VA: American Society of Group Psychotherapy and Psychodrama. Roanoke, VA: Royal Publishing Company.

Moreno, J. L., with Friedemann, A., Battegay, R. and Moreno, Z. T. (eds) (1966) *The International Handbook of Group Psychotherapy*. New York: Philosophical Library.

Moreno, J. L., Jennings, H. H., Criswell, J. H., Katz, L., Blake, R. R., Mouton, J. S., Bonney, M. S., Northway, M. L., Loomis, C. P., Procter, C., Tagiuri, R. and Nehnevajsa, J. (eds) (1960) *The Sociometry Reader*. Glencoe, IL: Free Press.

Moreno, J. L. and Moreno, F. B. (1944) "Spontaneity theory of child development", *Sociometry*, 7: 89–128.

Moreno, J. L., with Moreno, Z. T. (1959) *Psychodrama, Second Volume: Foundations of Psychotherapy*. Beacon, NY: Beacon House.

Moreno, J. L., with Moreno, Z. T. (1969) *Psychodrama, Third Volume: Action Therapy and Principles of Practice*. Beacon, NY: Beacon House.

Moreno, J. L., Moreno, Z. T. and Moreno, J. (1964) *The First Psychodramatic Family*. Beacon, NY: Beacon House.

References

Anthony, E. J. (1971) "The history of group psychotherapy", in H. I. Kaplan and B. J. Sadock (eds), *Comprehensive Group Psychotherapy*. Baltimore: Williams and Wilkins. pp. 4–31.

Bales, R. F. (1950) *Interaction Process Analysis: a Method for the Study of Small Groups*. Cambridge, MA: Addison-Wesley.

Berger, M. M. (1990) "J. L. Moreno's autobiography: more than meets the eye", *Journal of Group Psychotherapy, Psychodrama and Sociometry*, 42(4): 213–21.

Berne, E. (1970) "A review of *Gestalt Therapy Verbatim*", *American Journal of Psychiatry*, 126(10): 164.

Bischof, L. J. (1970) *Interpreting Personality Theories*, 2nd edn. New York: Harper & Row.

Bjerstedt, A. (1963) [*Sociometric Methods.*] Uppsala: Almqvist and Wiksell.

Blake, R. R. and McCanse, A. A. (1989) "The rediscovery of sociometry", *Journal of Group Psychotherapy, Psychodrama and Sociometry*, 42(3): 148–65.

Blatner, H. [A.] (1968) "Comments on some commonly held reservations about psychodrama", *Group Psychotherapy*, 21(1): 20–5.

Blatner, H. A. (1973) *Acting-in: Practical Applications of Psychodramatic Methods*. New York: Springer.

Blatner, [H.] A. and Blatner, A. (1988) *Foundations of Psychodrama: History, Theory, and Practice*. New York: Springer.

Borgatta, E. F. (1968) "Sociometry", in D. L. Sills (ed.), *International Encyclopedia of the Social Sciences*, vol. 15. New York: Macmillan and Free Press. pp. 53–7.

Borgatta, E. F., Boguslaw, R. and Haskell, M. R. (1975) "On the work of Jacob L. Moreno", *Sociometry*, 38(1): 148–61.

Bramel, D. (1969) "Interpersonal attraction, hostility, and perception", in J. Mills (ed.), *Experimental Social Psychology*. New York: Macmillan. pp. 3–10.

Bruch, M. (1954) "An example of the use of psychodrama in the relieving of an acute symptom in a psychiatric children's clinic", *Group Psychotherapy*, 6(3–4): 216–21.

Byrne, D. and Griffitt, W. (1973) "Interpersonal attraction", *Annual Review of Psychology*, 24: 317–36.

Corey, G. (1985) *Theory and Practice of Group Counseling*, 2nd edn. Pacific Grove, CA: Brooks/Cole.

Cottrell, L. S. and Goodenough, R. G. (1941) "Developments in social psychology, 1930–1940", *Sociometry Monograph*, 1.

Cramer-Azima, F. J. (1990) "Moreno – a personal reflection", *Journal of Group Psychotherapy, Psychodrama and Sociometry*, 42(4): 222–4.

Dreikurs, R. and Corsini, R. J. (1954) "Twenty years of group psychotherapy", *American Journal of Psychiatry*, 110: 567–75.

Fox, J. (ed.) (1987) *The Essential Moreno*. New York: Springer.

Fox, J. (1995) *Acts of Service: Spontaneity, Commitment, Tradition in the Nonscripted Theater*. New Paltz, NY: Tusitala Publishing.

Fromm-Reichmann, F. and Moreno, J. L. (eds) (1956) *Progress in Psychotherapy*. New York: Grune and Stratton.

Fuhlrodt, R. L. (ed.) (1990) *Psychodrama: its Application to Acoa and Substance Abuse Treatment*. East Rutherford, NJ: Perrin.

Glanzer, M. and Glazer, R. (1959) "Techniques for the study of group structure and behavior: I. Analysis of structure", *Psychological Bulletin*, 56(5): 317–32.

Goldman, E. and Morrison, D. S. (1984) *Psychodrama: Experience and Process*. Dubuque, IA: Kendall/Hunt.

Greenberg, I. A. (ed.) (1974) *Psychodrama: Theory and Therapy*. New York: Behavioral Publications.

Guldner, C. A. (ed.) (1990a) "Theme issue: psychodrama and sociometry in university education", *Journal of Group Psychotherapy, Psychodrama and Sociometry*, 43(2).

Guldner, C. A. (ed.) (1990b) "Theme issue: psychodrama and group work with adolescents," *Journal of Group Psychotherapy, Psychodrama and Sociometry*, 43(3).

Hale, A. E. (1985) *Conducting Clinical Sociometric Explorations*. Roanoke, VA: Royal Publishing Company.

Hare, A. P. (1976) *Handbook of Small Group Research*. New York: Free Press.

Hare, A. P. (1979) "Moreno, Jacob L.", in D. L. Sills (ed.), *International Encyclopedia of the Social Sciences*, vol. 18. New York: Macmillan. pp. 537–41.

Hare, A. P. (1982) *Creativity in Small Groups*. Beverly Hills, CA: Sage.

Hare, A. P. (1985) *Social Interaction as Drama*. Beverly Hills, CA: Sage.

Hare, A. P. (1986a) "Bibliography of the work of J. L. Moreno", *Journal of Group Psychotherapy, Psychodrama and Sociometry*, 39(3): 95–128.

Hare, A. P. (1986b) "Moreno's contribution to social psychology", *Journal of Group Psychotherapy, Psychodrama and Sociometry*, 39(3): 85–94.

Hare, A. P. (1992) "Moreno's sociometric study at the Hudson School for Girls", *Journal of Group Psychotherapy, Psychodrama, and Sociometry*, 45(1): 24–39.

Hare, A. P. (1994) "Types of roles in small groups", *Small Group Research*, 25: 433–48.

Hare, A. P. and Blumberg, H. H. (1988) *Dramaturgical Analysis of Social Interaction*. New York: Praeger.

Hare, A. P., Blumberg, H. H., Davies, M. F. and Kent, M. V. (1994) *Small Group Research: a Handbook*. Norwood, NJ: Ablex Publishing.

Hart, J. E. (ed.) (1987) "Special issue on sociometry", *Journal of Group Psychotherapy, Psychodrama and Sociometry*, 40(3).

Haskell, M. R. (1975) *Socioanalysis: Self-direction via Sociometry and Psychodrama*. Los Angeles, CA: Role Training Associates of California.

Holmes, P. and Karp, M. (1991) *Psychodrama: Inspiration and Technique*. London: Tavistock/Routledge.

Holmes, P., Karp, M. and Watson, M. (eds) (1994) *Psychodrama since Moreno: Innovations in Theory and Practice*. London: Routledge.

Jennings, H. H. (1960) "Sociometric choice process in personality and group formation", in J. L. Moreno et al. (eds), *The Sociometry Reader*. Glencoe, IL: Free Press. pp. 87–112.

Kahn, S. (1964) *Psychodrama Explained*. New York: Philosophical Library.

Kane, R. (1992) "The potential abuses, limitations, and negative effects of classical psychodramatic techniques in group counseling", *Journal of Group Psychotherapy, Psychodrama and Sociometry*, 44(4): 181–9.

Kellermann, P. F. (1987) "Outcome research in classical psychodrama", *Small Group Behavior*, 18(4): 459–69.

Kellermann, P. F. (1991) "An essay on the metascience of psychodrama", *Journal of Group Psychotherapy, Psychodrama and Sociometry*, 44(1): 19–32.

Kellermann, P. F. (1992) *Focus on Psychodrama: the Therapeutic Aspects of Psychodrama*. London: Jessica Kingsley.

Kelley, H. H., Berscheid, E., Christensen, A., Harvey, J. H., Huston, T. L., Levinger, G., McClintock, E., Peplau, L. A. and Peterson, D. R. (1983) *Close Relationships*. New York: Freeman.

Kipper, D. A. (1978) "Trends in the research on the effectiveness of psychodrama: retrospect and prospect", *Group Psychotherapy, Psychodrama and Sociometry*, 31: 5–18.

Kipper, D. A. (1986) *Psychotherapy through Clinical Roleplaying*. New York: Brunner/Mazel.

Kipper, D. A. (1988) "On the definition of psychodrama: another view", *Journal of Group Psychotherapy, Psychodrama and Sociometry*, 40(4): 164–8.

Kreitler, H. and Elblinger, S. (1961) "Psychiatric and cultural aspects of the opposition to psychodrama", *Group Psychotherapy*, 14(3-4): 215–20.

Landy, R. J. (1986) *Drama Therapy: Concepts and Practices*. Springfield, IL: Charles C. Thomas.

Langley, D. M. and Langley, G. E. (1983) *Dramatherapy and Psychiatry*. London: Croom Helm.

Leveton, E. (1977) *Psychodrama for the Timid Clinician*. New York: Springer.

Levinger, G. (1980) "Toward the analysis of close relationships", *Journal of Experimental Social Psychology*, 16: 510–44.

Lindzey, G. and Borgatta, E. F. (1954) "Sociometric measurement", in G. Lindzey and E. Aronson (eds), *Handbook of Social Psychology*. Reading, MA: Addison-Wesley. pp. 405–48.

Lindzey, G. and Byrne, D. (1968) "Measurement of social choice and interpersonal attractiveness", in G. Lindzey and E. Aronson (eds), *Handbook of Social Psychology*. Reading, MA: Addison-Wesley. pp. 452–525.

Marineau, R. F. (1989) *Jacob Levy Moreno 1889–1974: Father of Psychodrama, Sociometry, and Group Psychotherapy*. London: Tavistock/Routledge.

Maslow, A. H. (1968) "Letter to the Editor", *LIFE Magazine*.

Masserman, J. L. and Moreno, J. L. (eds) (1957–60) *Progress in Psychotherapy*. New York: Grune and Stratton.

Mead, G. H. (1950) *Mind, Self, and Society*. Chicago: University of Chicago Press.

Mendelson, P. (1989) "The sociometric vision", *Journal of Group Psychotherapy, Psychodrama and Sociometry*, 42(3): 138–47.

Meyer, H. J. (1952) "The sociometries of Dr Moreno", *Sociometry*, 15: 354–63.

Moreno, J. L. (1914–15) *Einladung zu einer Begegnung* [An invitation to a meeting]. Vienna: Anzengruber Verlag.

Moreno, J. L. (1919) "Die Gottheit als Redner" [The Godhead as orator/preacher], *Daimon*, 2: 1–19.

Moreno, J. L. (1923a) *Das Stegreiftheater* [The theater of spontaneity]. Berlin–Potsdam: Kiepenheuer Verlag.

Moreno, J. L. (1923b) *Der Koenigsroman* [The king's novel]. Potsdam: Kiepenheuer Verlag.

Moreno, J. L. (1934) *Who Shall Survive? A New Approach to the Problem of Human Interrelations.* Washington, DC: Nervous and Mental Disease Publishing Co.

Moreno, J. L. (ed.) (1945a) *Group Psychotherapy: a Symposium.* Beacon, NY: Beacon House.

Moreno, J. L. (1945b) "Sociometry, Comtism and Marxism", *Sociometry*, 8: 117–19.

Moreno, J. L. (1947a) "Progress and pitfalls in sociometric theory", *Sociometry*, 10(3): 268–72.

Moreno, J. L. (1947b) "Sociometry and the social psychology of G. H. Mead", *Sociometry*, 10(4): 350–3.

Moreno, J. L. (1947c) *The Theatre of Spontaneity.* Beacon, NY: Beacon House. (Reprinted as third edition in 1980.)

Moreno, J. L. (1949a) "Origins and foundations of interpersonal theory, sociometry and microsociology", *Sociometry*, 12(1–3): 235–54.

Moreno, J. L. (1949b) "Sociometry and Marxism", *Sociometry*, 12(1–3): 106–43.

Moreno, J. L. (1951a) "Fragments from the psychodrama of a dream", *Group Psychotherapy*, 3(4): 344–64.

Moreno, J. L. (1951b) *Sociometry, Experimental Method and the Science of Society.* Beacon, NY: Beacon House.

Moreno, J. L. (1952) "Current trends in sociometry", *Sociometry*, 15(1–2): 146–63.

Moreno, J. L. (1953) *Who Shall Survive? Foundations of Sociometry, Group Psychotherapy, and Sociodrama.* Beacon, NY: Beacon House. (Revised from 1934 edition. Reprinted as third edition in 1978.)

Moreno, J. L. (1954) "Old and new trends in sociometry: turning points in small group research", *Sociometry*, 17(2): 179–93.

Moreno, J. L. (1955a) "Psychodrama", in J. L. McCary and D. E. Sheer (eds), *Six Approaches to Psychotherapy.* New York: Dryden. pp. 289–340.

Moreno, J. L. (1955b) "System of spontaneity–creativity–conserve: a reply to P. Sorokin", *Sociometry*, 18(4): 382–92.

Moreno, J. L. (1955c) "The birth of a new era for sociometry", *Sociometry*, 18(4): 261–8.

Moreno, J. L. (1955d) "The sociometric school and the science of man", *Sociometry*, 18(4): 271–91.

Moreno, J. L. (1955e) "Theory of spontaneity–creativity", *Sociometry*, 18(4): 361–74.

Moreno, J. L. (1956) *Sociometry and the Science of Man.* Beacon, NY: Beacon House.

Moreno, J. L. (1957a) "Psychodrama", in J. E. Fairchild (ed.), *Personal Problems and Psychological Frontiers.* New York: Sheridan House.

Moreno, J. L. (1957b) *The First Book on Group Psychotherapy: 1932.* Beacon, NY: Beacon House.

Moreno, J. L. (1958) "Comments [on the history of psychodrama]", *Group Psychotherapy*, 11(3): 260.

Moreno, J. L. (1959a) *Gruppenpsychotherapie und Psychodrama: Einleitung in die Theorie und Praxis.* Stuttgart: Thième.

Moreno, J. L. (1959b) "Psychodrama," in S. Arieti (ed.), *American Handbook of Psychiatry.* New York: Basic Books. pp. 1375–96.

Moreno, J. L. (1961) "Psychodrama and sociodrama of Judaism and the Eichmann trial", *Group Psychotherapy*, 14(1–2): 114–16.

Moreno, J. L. (1964a) "Psychodrama of murder, a joint trial of Lee Harvey Oswald and Jack Ruby", *Group Psychotherapy*, 17(1): 61–2.

Moreno, J. L. (1964b) "The third psychiatric revolution and the scope of psychodrama", *Group Psychotherapy*, 17(2–3): 149–71.

Moreno, J. L. (1967) "Psychodrama," in A. M. Freedman and H. I. Kaplan (eds), *Comprehensive Textbook of Psychiatry*. Baltimore: Williams and Wilkins.

Moreno, J. L. (1970) "The triadic system, psychodrama–sociometry–group psychotherapy", *Group Psychotherapy and Psychodrama*, 23(1–2): 16.

Moreno, J. L. (1971) *The Words of the Father*. Beacon, NY: Beacon House. (First published 1941.)

Moreno, J. L. (1972) *Psychodrama: First Volume*. Beacon, NY: Beacon House. (First edition 1946.)

Moreno, J. L. (1973) "Note on indications and contra-indications for acting out in psychodrama", *Group Psychotherapy and Psychodrama*, 26(1–2): 23–4.

Moreno, J. L. (1985) *Autobiography* (cited in Marineau, 1989).

Moreno, J. L. (1989a) "The autobiography of J. L. Moreno, MD" (edited by J. D. Moreno), *Journal of Group Psychotherapy, Psychodrama and Sociometry*, 42(1): 2–52.

Moreno, J. L. (1989b) "The autobiography of J. L. Moreno, MD" (edited by J. D. Moreno), *Journal of Group Psychotherapy, Psychodrama and Sociometry*, 42(2): 59–126.

Moreno, J. L. (1993) *Who Shall Survive?* (student edition, edited by Ann Hale). McLean, VA: American Society of Group Psychotherapy and Psychodrama. Roanoke, VA: Royal Publishing Company.

Moreno, J. L. and Borgatta, E. F. (1951) "An experiment with sociodrama and sociometry in industry", *Sociometry* , 14(1): 71–104.

Moreno, J. L. and Dunkin, W. S. (1941) "The function of the social investigator in experimental psychodrama", *Sociometry*, 4: 392–417.

Moreno, J. L. and Enneis, J. M. (1950) "Hypnodrama and psychodrama", *Psychodrama Monographs*, no. 27.

Moreno, J. L., with Friedemann, A., Battegay, R. and Moreno, Z. T. (eds) (1966) *The International Handbook of Group Psychotherapy*. New York: Philosophical Library.

Moreno, J. L. and Jennings, H. H. (1938) "Statistics of social configurations", *Sociometry*, 1: 342–74.

Moreno, J. L., Jennings, H. H., Criswell, J. H., Katz, L., Blake, R. R., Mouton, J. S., Bonney, M. S., Northway, M. L., Loomis, C. P., Procter, C., Tagiuri, R. and Nehnevajsa, J. (eds) (1960) *The Sociometry Reader*. Glencoe, IL: Free Press.

Moreno, J. L., Jennings, H. H. and Sargent, J. (1940) "Time as a quantitative index of inter-personal relations", *Sociometry*, 3: 62–80.

Moreno, J. L., with Jennings, H. H. and Stockton, R. (1943) "Sociometry in the classroom", *Sociometry*, 6: 425–8.

Moreno, J. L. and Moreno, F. B. (1944) "Spontaneity theory of child development", *Sociometry*, 7: 89–128.

Moreno, J. L., with Moreno, Z. T. (1959) *Psychodrama, Second Volume: Foundations of Psychotherapy*. Beacon, NY: Beacon House.

Moreno, J. L., with Moreno, Z. T. (1969) *Psychodrama, Third Volume: Action Therapy and Principles of Practice*. Beacon, NY: Beacon House.

Moreno, J. L., Moreno, Z. T. and Moreno, J. (1964) *The First Psychodramatic Family*. Beacon, NY: Beacon House.

Moreno, J. L. and Toeman, Z. (1942) "The group approach in psychodrama", *Sociometry*, 5: 191–6.

Moreno, Z. T. (1965) "Psychodramatic rules, techniques, and adjunctive methods", *Group Psychotherapy*, 18: 73–86.

Moreno, Z. T. (1969a) "Moreneans, the heretics of yesterday are the orthodoxy of today", *Group Psychotherapy*, 22(1–2): 1–6.

Moreno, Z. T. (1969b) "The seminal mind of J. L. Moreno and his influence upon the present generation", in J. L. Moreno, with Z. T. Moreno, *Psychodrama, Third Volume: Action Therapy and Principles of Practice*. Beacon, NY: Beacon House. pp. 247–58.

Moreno, Z. T. (1976) "In memoriam: J. L. Moreno", *Group Psychotherapy, Psychodrama and Sociometry*, 29: 130–5.

Moreno, Z. T. (1978) "Psychodrama", in H. Mullan and M. Rosenbaum (eds), *Group Psychotherapy: Theory and Practice*, 2nd edn. New York: Free Press.

Moreno, Z. T. (1983) "Psychodrama", in H. I. Kaplan and B. J. Sadock (eds), *Comprehensive Group Psychotherapy*, 2nd edn. Baltimore: Williams and Wilkins.

Murphy, G. and Murphy, L. B. (1931) *Experimental Social Psychology*. New York: Harper.

Nehnevajsa, J. (1956) "Sociometry: decades of growth", in J. L. Moreno (ed.), *Sociometry and the Science of Man*. Beacon, NY: Beacon House. pp. 48–95.

Nolte, J. (1989) "Remembering J. L. Moreno", *Journal of Group Psychotherapy, Psychodrama and Sociometry*, 42(3): 129–37.

Rabson, J. S. (1979) *Psychodrama: Theory and Method*. Cape Town: University of Cape Town, Department of Sociology.

Remer, R. (1995) "Strong sociometry: a definition," *Journal of Group Psychotherapy, Psychodrama and Sociometry*, 48(2): 69–74.

Rockwell, T. (1987) "The social construction of careers: career development and career counseling viewed from a sociometric perspective", *Journal of Group Psychotherapy, Psychodrama and Sociometry*, 40(3): 93–107.

Roethlisberger, F. J. and Dickson, W. J. (1939) *Management and the Worker*. Cambridge, MA: Harvard University Press.

Sahakian, W. S. (ed.) (1972) *Social Psychology: Experimentation, Theory, Research*. Scranton, PA: Intext Educational Publishers. pp. 156–63.

Salas, J. (1993) *Improvising Real Life: Personal Story in Playback Theatre*. Dubuque, IA: Kendall/Hunt.

Sasson, F. (1990) "Psychodrama with adolescents: management techniques that work", *Journal of Group Psychotherapy, Psychodrama and Sociometry*, 43(3): 121–7.

Schutz, W. (1971) *Here Comes Everybody*. New York: Harper and Row.

Shaffer, J. B. P. and Galinsky, M. D. (1974) *Models of Group Therapy and Sensitivity Training*. Englewood Cliffs, NJ: Prentice-Hall.

Shoobs, N. E. (1956) "Role-playing in the individual psychotherapy interview", *Journal of Individual Psychology*, 20(1): 84–9.

Sorokin, P. A. (1949) "Concept, tests, and energy of spontaneity–creativity", *Sociometry*, 12(1–3): 215–24.

Sorokin, P. A. (1955) "Remarks on J. L. Moreno's 'theory of spontaneity and creativity'", *Sociometry*, 18(4): 374–82.

Starr, A. (1977) *Rehearsal for Living: Psychodrama*. Chicago: Nelson Hall.

Sternberg, P. and Garcia, A. (1989) *Sociodrama: Who's in your Shoes?* New York: Praeger.

Stein, M. B. and Callahan, M. L. (1982) "The use of psychodrama in individual psychotherapy", *Journal of Group Psychotherapy, Psychodrama, and Sociometry*, 35(3): 118–29.

Strodtbeck, F. L. and Hare, A. P. (1954) "Bibliography of small group research (from 1900 through 1953)", *Sociometry*, 17(2): 107–78.

Swanson, G. E., Newcomb, T. M. and Hartley, E. L. (eds) (1952) *Readings in Social Psychology*. New York: Henry Holt.

Toeman, Z. (1949) "History of the sociometric movement in headlines", *Sociometry*, 12(1–3): 255–9.

Treadwell, T. W., Stein, S. and Kumar, V. K. (1990) "A survey of psychodramatic action and closure techniques", *Journal of Psychotherapy, Psychodrama and Sociometry*, 43(3): 102–15.

Walton, H. (ed.) (1971) *Small Group Psychotherapy*. Harmondsworth: Penguin.

Warner, W. J. (1954) "Sociology and psychiatry", *The British Journal of Sociology*, 5(3): 228–37.

Wellman, M. (1963) "Basic principles of Moreno's contribution to psychology", *Group Psychotherapy*, 16(4): 260–84.

Whyte, W. F. (1943) *Street Corner Society*. Chicago: University of Chicago Press.

von Wiese, L. (1949) "Sociometry", *Sociometry*, 12(1–3): 202–14.

Williams, A. (1989) *The Passionate Technique: Strategic Psychodrama with Individuals, Families, and Groups*. London: Tavistock/Routledge.

Wolson, P. (1971) "Loss of impulse control in psychodrama on inpatient services", *Handbook of International Sociometry*, 6: 73–83.

Yablonsky, L. (1968) "Psychodrama and sociometry: an appraisal", in I. A. Greenberg (ed.), *Psychodrama and Audience Attitude Change*. Beverly Hills, CA: Behavioral Studies Press. pp. 239–48.

Yablonsky, L. (1976) *Psychodrama: Resolving Emotional Problems through Role-Playing*. New York: Basic Books.

Name Index

Ackerman, N. W. 99
Adler, A. 21, 100
Allport, G. A. 99
Anthony, E. J. 87

Bain, R. 102
Bales, R. F. 43
Beecher, B. 16
Benne, K. 21
Berger, M. M. 18
Berne, E. 110
Bischof, L. J. 27, 40
Bjerstedt, A. 109
Blake, R. R. 102, 109
Blakeslee, H. 18
Blatner, A. 30, 71, 91, 111, 112
Blatner, H. A. 30, 71, 87, 89, 91, 111, 112
Block, E. 14
Blumberg, H. H. 38
Boguslaw, R. 21, 118
Bonney, M. E. 21
Borgatta, E. F. 21, 41, 96, 97, 109, 117, 118, 119
Boss, M. 103
Bradford, L. 21
Bramel, D. 109
Bridge, F. 19, 25
Brill, A. A. 18
Brod, M. 14
Bromberg, W. 99
Bruch, M. 70
Buber, M. 14
Byrne, D. 109

Callahan, M. L. 40
Cholden, L. 101
Colbert, C. 8
Comte, A. 88

Corey, G. 93
Corsini, R. J. 116
Cottrell, L. S. 113
Cramer-Azima, F. J. 24

Darwin, C. 7
Dickson, W. J. 42
Dreikurs, R. 116
Dunkin, W. S. 69

Eherenstein, A. 14
Elblinger, S. 91
Enneis, J. M. 21, 68

Fox, J. 55, 107, 111
Freud, S. 7, 15, 27, 88, 100, 101, 120
Froebel, F. 23
Fromm-Reichmann, F. 22, 102, 111
Fuhlrodt, R. L. 111

Galinsky, M. D. 104, 111, 112
Garcia, A. 111
Glanzer, M. 109
Glazer, R. 109
Goldman, E. 111
Goodenough, R. G. 113
Greenberg, I. A. 93, 111
Greun, W. 8
Griffitt, W. 109
Guldner, C. A. 111
Gurvitch, G. 22, 88

Haas, R. 21
Hale, A. E. 109, 111
Hare, A. P. 24, 38, 39, 42, 43, 72, 89, 109, 121
Hart, J. E. 109
Hartley, E. L. 41
Haskell, M. R. 21, 111, 119

132   *J. L. Moreno*

Holmes, P. 111
Homans, G. C. 88

Iancu, P. 2

James, R. 101
Jammes, F. 14
Jennings, H. H. 17, 18, 25, 41, 42, 103, 104
Jung, C. G. 100

Kahn, S. 111
Kaiser, G. 14
Kane, R. 40, 93
Karp, M. 111
Kellermann, P. F. 93, 94, 95, 111
Kelley, H. H. 109
Kellmer, C. 6
Kennedy, J. F. 63
Kipper, D. A. 91, 95, 111
Kolaja, J. 103
Kreitler, H. 91

Landy, R. J. 93
Langley, D. M. 93
Langley, G. E. 93
Leveton, E. 111
Levinger, G. 109
Levy, M. N. 2
Levy, R. 21
Lindzey, G. 96, 97, 109
Lippitt, R. 21
Loomis, C. 19
Loomis, E. A. 99
Lörnitzo, F. 16
Lörnitzo, M. 10, 15, 17
Lundberg, G. 19

Mann, H. 14
Marianne (Lörnitzo) 10, 15, 17
Marx, K. 7, 15, 27, 88
Marineau, R. F. 2, 3, 4, 7, 9, 10, 11, 12, 13, 14, 15, 16, 19, 20, 24
Maslow, A. H. 110
Masserman, J. H. 22, 99, 111
McCanse, A. A. 109
Mead, G. H. 38, 88, 112, 113
Mendelson, P. 109
Meyer, H. J. 104, 113, 114, 115
Moreno, F. B. 25, 39

Moreno, J. (Jonathan) 20, 102
Moreno, J. L., works
(1914–15) 14
(1919) 12
(1923a) 15
(1923b) 14
(1934) 1, 2, 18, 32, 41, 96, 103, 104
(1938, with Jennings) 41
(1940, with Jennings and Sargent) 41
(1941, with Dunkin) 69
(1942, with Toeman) 20
(1943, with Jennings and Stockton) 41
(1944, with F. B. Moreno) 39
(1945a) 20, 111
(1945b) 88
(1947a) 41
(1947b) 88
(1947c) 15
(1949a) 88
(1949b) 88
(1950, with Enneis) 68
(1951a) 55
(1951b) 88, 104, 113
(1951, with Borgatta) 41
(1952) 41
(1953) 1, 6, 8, 23, 24, 26, 27, 29, 31, 33, 35, 38, 41, 43, 45, 57, 58, 72, 73, 74, 77, 80, 81, 83, 87, 103, 104, 113, 115
(1954) 42
(1955a) 111
(1955b) 88
(1955c) 42
(1955d) 41
(1955e) 88
(1956) 41, 44, 87, 88
(1956, with Fromm-Reichmann) 22, 102, 111
(1957a) 111
(1957b) 18, 24
(1957–60, with Masserman) 22, 111
(1958) 3
(1959a) 23
(1959b) 111
(1959, with Z. Moreno) 29, 42, 97
(1960, et al.) 27, 30, 31, 32, 33, 34, 35, 36, 38, 41, 42, 109
(1961) 62
(1964a) 63

Subject Index